The Mountain Traveller's Handbook

Your companion from city to summit

Paul Deegan

Contents

Notes For The Reader

The Definitive Resource

With more than 60 advisors and contributors (most of whom are the acknowledged leaders in their respective fields of medicine, expedition logistics, leadership, mountain guiding, photography and filming) this book is the definitive resource for anyone heading to the mountain environment. There is a special focus on subjects such as the environment, mountain communities and traditional cultures, and this has been recognised by organisations such as the United Nations' International Year of Mountains, the International Porter Protection Group and the Access & Conservation Trust. Proceeds from the book will be directed towards the work of the British Mountaineering Council (BMC) in areas such as access and conservation. The BMC is confident that The Mountain Traveller's Handbook will become the standard work on travel in the high mountains. Thank you for buying this book.

Terminology

The terms 'Trekker', 'Backpacker' and 'Mountaineer' have been used extensively throughout this book. 'Trekker' and 'Backpacker' denote anyone who walks in the mountains, whether independently or with a guide, and who does not intend to tackle any ground that would require the accoutrements of the mountaineer (such as helmet, rope and harness). The term also encompasses people who wish to make ascents of technically straightforward mountains such as Kilimanjaro and Cerro Aconcagua. 'Mountaineer' is used to describe rock climbers, alpinists and climbers who are already familiar with the techniques and equipment required to ascend steep terrain. It is worth noting that occasionally the word 'climb' is used colloquially to describe routes of ascent that are also suitable for the trekker.

Safety

At the time of writing, some of the mountains referred to in this book were deemed by the Travel Advice Unit of the Foreign & Commonwealth Office to be unsafe for foreigners to visit. All references to individual mountain regions should not be interpreted as a recommendation to visit. Readers are strongly advised to make their own enquiries as to the security situation in their intended destination before setting out. *Appendix A contains contact details for organisations that can advise on the safety of the country you are visiting.*

Other Notes

The spelling of certain geographical names may appear unfamiliar to some readers. For example, the generally accepted 'Himalayas' is replaced in this book by 'Himalaya' to reflect the fact that it is a single mountain range. Some places have more than one correct spelling. In these instances, the most commonly used version has been used. For the sake of uniformity only, the male gender has been used exclusively throughout this book when referring to the individual, with the exception of the section on additional considerations for women in Chapter 11.

Who This Book Is For

Whilst no publication can hope to replace the lessons learnt through personal experience, this book provides the first-timer with the minimum amount of information required to steer a safer and more enjoyable course through the mountains. After all, a trek in the Himalaya or an ascent of an easy-angled 5000 metre peak are mighty places indeed in which to act out your mountain apprenticeship. For the trekker or mountaineer already familiar with the rudiments of the mountain game, but who has yet to venture to foreign shores, the chapters cover all the new skills that you will want to acquaint yourself with, from avoiding altitude sickness to tipping porters. Whilst it is fair to say that this book has been written with the more independent traveller in mind, most of what is useful for people who choose to go it alone is also relevant to the person who decides to join a commercial trip. For example, your guide may well be a native of the country that you are visiting. Whilst his local knowledge will undoubtedly enrich your experience, it might be awkward for him to explain certain things (such as what constitutes appropriate trekking attire) for fear of insulting you, the paying client. Armed with the information in this book, you will be able to give yourself the opportunity to see the mountains that you visit through the eyes of your host, and not just your own.

How To Use This Book

This book has been designed to be read either from cover-to-cover or one chapter at a time in any order. Certain chapters naturally pair up together. For example, it is useful to read the chapter on drinking and eating with the chapter on altitude illness, as the amount that you drink will often have a great bearing on how you perform in the high mountains. The description of a typical mountain day appears early on in the book for readers who have yet to spend time trekking. By gaining an early appreciation of what is involved, the reader will appreciate the importance of subjects such as medical kits and clothing which follow later on in the book. Each chapter has one or more information boxes that can be read either on its own or as part of the chapter. A question and answer box can be found at the end of each chapter. References to other parts of the book are made in italics at the end of the appropriate paragraph.

We Welcome Your Comments

The author and the BMC welcome your comments on any aspect of the book. Please email: paul@mountaintravellershandbook.com or write to Paul Deegan c/o the BMC.

Participation Statement

'Trekkers, mountaineers and the BMC recognise that participation in mountain activities is inherently risky. You should only get involved in these activities if you are personally prepared to accept these risks and recognise that you will be exposed to potentially life-threatening situations.'

Acknowledgements

Firstly, I would like to express my gratitude to the dozens of highly experienced mountaineers, trekkers and other professionals who responded to my request for contributions, and replied with the many words of wisdom that can be found throughout the book.

Behind-the-scenes, Roger Astley, John Barry, Jeneatte Davey, Ken Daynes OBE, Gaby Dean, Steve Duffy, Katrina Halliday, Rob Halliday, Andy Hodgkinson, Stuart Ingram, Alex Messenger, Angus Murray, Tim Salmon, Kathryn Smith, Peter Stewart and Ken Vickers gave much-needed support and advice.

The main body of text speaks with a single voice but contains the thoughts and experiences of more than 40 people. I would like to extend my thanks to: George Band, Mike Banks, Al Boardman, Dave Bradbrook, Liz Carritt, Phil Coates, John Cousins, Karen Darke, Jo Farrington, Becky Foster, Paul Goodyer, Ted Gray, Lindsay Griffin, Vivian Grisogono, Anna Grove, Simon Harris-Ward, Martin Hartley, Dan Haylock, Steve Jones, Jaj Kang, Nick Lewis, George Lowe, Andy Miles, Martin Price, Glenn Shaw, Giles Stumpe, Jon Tinker, Chris Trevallion, Darren Tulley, Larry Tyson, Phil Waters, Steve Watkins, Steve Webster, Dan White, Kjersti Winger, Shane Winser and Marek Zielinski.

A number of doctors gave freely of their time. I would not have been able to write the medical and high altitude chapters without the assistance I received from Dr John Mitchell and Dr David Hillebrandt. In addition, Dr Jane Wilson-Howarth educated me on issues for women and children, Dr Jim Duff brought me up-to-date on pressure chambers and porter welfare, and Dr Ryck Albertyn assisted with the sections on rescue, repatriation and insurance.

I am particularly indebted to: Andy MacNae for giving me the opportunity to write this book; Seb Mankelow for his valuable input during the initial phases of the project and for his thoughts on over half the chapters; and Ros – for being my guide.

Certain aspects of the nutritional information in Chapters 3 and 11 have been re-printed with kind permission from Jo Farrington's Glenmore Lodge/BMC workshop handouts. The examples of mountain tourism described in Chapter 16 were initially sourced from 'Mountains Of The World: Tourism And Sustainable Development', details of which can be found in Appendix E. The extract from Rudyard Kipling's 'The Explorer', appears by permission of A P Watt Ltd., on behalf of the National Trust for Places of Historical Interest or Natural Beauty.

Paul Deegan
Chamonix Valley

For Mum and Dad. For everything.

> *Something hidden. Go and find it. Go and look behind the Ranges – Something lost behind the Ranges. Lost and waiting for you. Go!*
>
> *Rudyard Kipling, from 'The Explorer'*

The world's most famous alpine climb? Summit day on Mont Blanc

Your Mountain Adventure

From gentle treks along valley floors to high altitude ascents of snow-covered peaks, mountain travel is a broad church and everyone is welcome. You can make your journey as easy or as challenging as you wish. Options range from one-day excursions emanating from a mountain lodge to multi-week adventures carrying everything on your back. Whatever your ambitions, this book will help you achieve them.

WHERE TO GO?

Many people planning to spend a holiday in the mountains will have already chosen their destination; the deciding factor might have been a desire to see a particular peak, an interest in another culture or a determination to stand atop a summit. Sometimes it is all three and more besides.

For those of you who know that your next holiday must be in a high place (but no more than that) there is – quite literally – a world of possibilities. Whilst it would require another book to list them all, a continent-by-continent look at the world's mountains might serve as a starting point for your own investigations.

Think of Europe and most people think of the Alps. There are, however, dozens of other mountain regions worth exploring, from the Pyrenees of Spain to the Pindos mountains of Greece. Most Scandinavian countries have mile-upon-mile of deserted summits and tundra. The Tatras offer alpine climbing at a fraction of western European prices. Even southern European countries such as Portugal – which are often dismissed by trekkers and climbers as only suitable for sun-lovers – have their own pockets of highland, if you look hard enough for them.

Africa's mountains are crowned by Mount Kilimanjaro, the continent's highest point. 'Kili', together with its equatorial neighbours Mount Meru and Mount Kenya, offers both trekkers and mountaineers the opportunity to ascend from a sub-tropical to a sub-arctic environment in little more than a week (although whether it is wise to do so this quickly is open to debate). Yet Africa offers the mountain explorer much more than these sub-6000m peaks. Uganda's Ruwenzori, Ethiopia's Simien mountains, and Morocco's Atlas range – the last just a stone's throw from Europe – are just a few of the continent's less well-advertised mountain jewels.

The World Heritage site of Machu Picchu in Peru is a popular destination for mountain travellers

South America is home to the Andes, the world's longest and perhaps most diverse mountain range. Running for virtually the entire length of the continent, the Andes contains a lifetime's worth of opportunities for the backpacker and mountaineer. Highlights include Peru's Cordillera Blanca, Bolivia's Cordillera Real and Ecuador's high altitude volcanoes, as well as the region known as Patagonia which straddles southern Chile and Argentina.

North America contains a stunning choice of mountain ranges. The USA boasts the Sierra Nevada and the Cascades, as well as rock climbing meccas such as Yosemite and Joshua Tree. Canada is not short on mountain wilderness: backpacking opportunities abound in the infamous Yukon and the North West Territories, whilst the St. Elias range rivals the climbing in the adjoining American State of Alaska, which is one enormous playground for mountaineers. If you can't decide between America and Canada then head for North America's most renowned mountain range, the Rockies, which spans both countries.

Australasia's premier snow-capped mountains are to be found in New Zealand's Southern Alps, which offer alpinists technical climbing on mountains such as Cook, Tasman and Aspiring. Trekkers (or *trampers*, as they are known in New Zealand) are able to tackle world-class trails such as the Milford and Routeburn Tracks. Australia is perhaps less well-known for its mountains, but there are plenty of highland areas including the Snowy Mountains and Blue Mountains. The Carstensz Pyramid is perhaps the most well-known piece of rock in the Pacific, but there are gems here for the trekker too: the Kokoda Trail and the Shaggy Ridge in Papua New Guinea are tough treks steeped in the history of the Second World War.

Then there is Asia, home to the world's highest mountain range, the Himalaya. Bhutan, Tibet, Nepal, India and China all have a share of the thousands of peaks that make up the chain, and there remain many untrodden summits and valleys awaiting discovery. A number of other principle mountain ranges also vie for attention within Asia. The Karakoram is dominated by K2, the world's second-highest mountain, whilst Central Asia's Pamirs and Tien Shan ranges straddle the Central Independent States of the former Soviet Union and neighbouring China. Dozens of other locations, from the Hindu Kush to the Kamchatka volcanoes, await your discovery.

Finally, Antarctica has in recent years begun to reveal a new and frozen world of adventure in the Ellsworth Mountains and Queen Maud Land to those with the means to reach them. Meanwhile, the mountains that line the Antarctic Peninsula now offer increasingly affordable opportunities to climb on the Earth's most remote continent. It is interesting to note that Greenland has recently enjoyed a resurgence in popularity and is currently a very attractive destination for the adventurous mountain traveller eager for new challenges in an environment not dissimilar to Antarctica.

WHEN TO GO?

Deciding where to go is one thing, deciding when to go is quite another. The table on the following two pages will assist you in your quest to visit the perfect mountain destination at the optimum time of year.

> ‘When lifting your game from, say, climbing in the Alps to climbing in the Himalaya, don't be too ambitious. On you first Himalayan trip, set your sights low and aim for success.’
>
> *Steve Bell*

When To Go?

DESTINATION	JANUARY	FEBRUARY	MARCH	APRIL	MAY
France, Italy, Switzerland *European Alps and Pyrenees*	Winter alpine climbing, icefall climbing, skiing.				Some alpine climbing. Trekking below 2000m.
Europe, Middle East, North Africa *Selected regions*	Ski-touring and snowshoeing in Scandinavia (depending on latitude). Winter climbing in Tatras. Rock climbing in the Middle East.				Trekking in Morocco, Spain, Greece and Turkey.
Nepal *All areas*	Cold. Trekking possible at low elevations. High passes blocked by snow.			Trekking and climbing in all areas.	Too hot to trek at lower elevations.
Pakistan *Karakoram and Hindu Kush*	Trekking and mountaineering not recommended.		Long ski tours on glaciers above 4000m possible.		Trekking at lower elevations possible.
Bhutan *All areas*	Winter snows; trekking not recommended.		Some trekking possible.		
Indian Himalaya *All areas*	Winter snows, trekking not recommended.	Trekking in Indus Valley and Nubra sometimes possible.	Ski-mountaineering in Ladakh, Zanskar and Himachal Pradesh.		Trekking and climbing in Gangotri and Garhwal.
Tibet *Tibetan Plateau*	Trekking possible around Lhasa, Dringi and Shigatse. Other areas blocked by snow.		High passes blocked by snow.	Trekking in most areas.	Climbing and trekking possible.
Kyrgyz Republic, Tajikistan, Kazakhstan *Pamirs and Tien Shan*	Ski-mountaineering.		Trekking not recommended.		
Kenya and Tanzania *Kilimanjaro, Mt Kenya, Mt Meru*	Trekking and climbing in all areas.		Rainy season; trekking and climbing not recommended.		
Peru and Bolivia *Andes*	Trekking and climbing not recommended.				Best time for climbing and trekking.
Chile and Argentina *Patagonia and Aconcagua*	Trekking and climbing in all areas, including Aconcagua.			Some trekking in Patagonia possible.	As for June to September.
North America *Selected regions*	Winter alpine climbing, skiing. Rock climbing in the southern desert regions such as Joshua Tree.		Winter climbing, ski-mountaineering.	Ski-mountaineering opportunities.	Climbing in Alaska (best time for Denali).
New Zealand *Southern Alps*	Tramping and climbing in all areas.				Tramping possible, but expect snow on some routes.

JUNE	JULY	AUGUST	SEPTEMBER	OCTOBER	NOVEMBER	DECEMBER
Snow on high treks. Alpine climbing.	Trekking and summer alpine climbing.			Alpine climbing, but some huts and lifts shut.		Winter alpine climbing, skiing.
Trekking in Morocco, Spain, Greece and Turkey.	Trekking and mountaineering in Central Europe, Tatras, Austrian Alps and Scandinavia (e.g. Lyngen Alps).		Trekking in Scandinavia.		Rock climbing in Middle East.	Winter climbing in Tatras, rock climbing in Middle East.
Monsoon. Trekking and mountaineering not recommended, except in Dolpo and Mustang.				Trekking and mountaineering in all areas.		Trekking possible but expect snow above 4000m.
Late-lying snow on high treks.	Trekking and mountaineering possible.			Trekking and mountaineering not recommended.		
Monsoon; trekking not recommended.				Trekking in all areas.		
Trekking and climbing in most areas, but expect rain. Dry conditions more likely in Lahaul, Spiti, Ladakh, Zanskar and Northern Kinnaur.				Trekking and climbing in most areas except Gangotri, Ladakh and Zanskar.		
Climbing and trekking possible.	Trekking possible but expect rain or snow.		Trekking and climbing in all areas.			Trekking possible, but high passes blocked by snow.
Trekking and climbing in all areas.				Trekking and climbing not recommended.		Ski-mountaineering.
Trekking and climbing in all areas.				Rainy season; trekking not recommended.		Trekking and climbing in all areas.
Best time for climbing and trekking.			Some climbing and trekking in Southern Bolivia.	Trekking and climbing not recommended.		
Reasonably stable weather patterns in Patagonia, but winter snows make the region suitable only for experienced climbers and trekkers. Aconcagua not recommended.				Increasingly popular time for climbing in Patagonia.	Trekking and climbing in Patagonia possible.	Trekking and climbing in all areas, including Aconcagua.
Climbing in Alaska (best time for Denali).	Climbing across the entire continent. Wilderness trekking in Northern Canada, Yukon, NW Territories.		Best time for NE coast and desert plateaus.	Limited opportunities, with winter snows at high levels.		Winter alpine climbing, skiing. Rock climbing in Joshua Tree.
Ski-touring and ski-mountaineering possible. Certain trails (such as the Abel Tasman Coast Track) can be tramped at this time of year.					Tramping and climbing in all areas.	

HOW LONG TO GO FOR?

In theory it is possible to fly to Kathmandu, trek to a point within sight of
Mount Everest and be back at your place of work within a week. In reality,
a few more days would allow you to enjoy (rather than endure) the
experience. Calculating the correct number of days that are required to
complete a particular mountain journey safely and successfully can be
worked out by answering these three principal questions:

- How far away from your home is the country you wish to visit?
- What is the distance to the peak from the runway, road, or railhead?
- What altitude do you want to reach?

The number of hours (or days) it takes to travel to the country is important,
as the amount of time spent travelling to your destination can eat up much
of the time you have at your disposal. Two classic examples (for people
travelling from the UK) are the Southern Alps of New Zealand and
Patagonia in South America. Whilst the trekking in both of these stunning
areas takes place at comfortable low altitudes, the number of hours spent
flying to and from these locations makes a trip of less than three weeks
impractical to all but the most determined travellers.

When it comes to altitude, the restrictions are entirely physiological. It is
dangerous to expect the human body to adjust to heights above 2500m
without an appropriate period of acclimatisation. *You can read more about
the effects of altitude and the process of acclimatisation in Chapter 10.*

Another party of
trekkers reaches the
summit of Kilimanjaro

POPULAR MOUNTAIN DESTINATIONS

The following list highlights a small selection of the world's most popular treks and climbs, together with the recommended number of days required to complete them enjoyably (including air travel to and from the UK, and allowances for acclimatisation and some bad weather).

Aconcagua (climb) Argentina, 28 days

Annapurna Circuit (trek) Nepal, 28 days

Denali/Mt. McKinley (climb) Alaska, 26 days

Inca Trail & Machu Picchu (trek) Peru, 12 days

Imja Tse/Island Peak (climb) Nepal, 19 days

K2 Base Camp (trek) Pakistan, 23 days

Kilimanjaro & Mt. Kenya (climb) Tanzania & Kenya, 16 days

Mont Blanc (climb) France, 8 days

Tour of Mont Blanc (trek) France/Italy/Switzerland, 14 days

Bear in mind that on mountains that require a long approach trek, such as Imja Tse (Island Peak) the number of days spent on snow and ice might represent as little as 10% of the total time spent in-country. Notable exceptions to this general rule include mountains in places such as Alaska, Canada and Antarctica, where climbers are usually flown to the very foot of the peak that they wish to ascend. Destinations like these are a heaven-sent solution for people who only have a short holiday, but who nonetheless wish to attempt a long route on a remote mountain. *See page 124 for details of the Everest trek.*

'Plans alter so stay flexible. Seemingly unreasonable goals can be achieved but be prepared to ditch them in order to enjoy a more reasonable alternative. Be ready to make the most out of the situation you find yourself in.'

Henry Todd

Catch-Up Days

Treks and climbs are sometimes unavoidably extended by several days because of prolonged bad weather. Furthermore, flights can be cancelled due to high winds, roads can be washed away by landslides, leaves can make trails slippery… with all the possible delays that can occur, many experienced travellers prefer to build in one or two 'catch-up days' at the end of their journey so that they don't miss that all-important flight home. If you are unsure from the outset that you will be able to make the return flight, it might be worth paying slightly more for your airline ticket so that you can change the return date without incurring a large financial penalty.

THE WILDERNESS EXPERIENCE

Contrary to popular belief, many trekking routes do not take the backpacker into untouched mountain regions devoid of habitation. Indeed, some trails take the trekker along well-maintained paths that have been used for centuries to transport supplies between villages. Other routes, such as the Inca Trail to Machu Picchu in the Peruvian Andes, follow historic highways laid down by earlier civilisations. Even people on so-called 'remote' treks to countries like Tibet and Bhutan are likely to come across monasteries and hermitages. If you wish to experience total isolation, choose your trek with care and avoid the most popular mountain destinations at their busiest times of year.

ORGANISING YOUR TRIP

Once you have chosen where and when to go, one of the next things to decide is whether you want (or are required to have) the services of a commercial company. Your options include:

- Using a travel agency based in your home country
- Employing the services of an operator located in the country you are visiting (known as an 'in-country operator')
- Doing it all yourself

Each has its advantages and disadvantages. How much you want to arrange for yourself, whether you want to travel in a group and the size of your budget will help you decide which approach is right for you. You could end up using a mix of two (or on occasion all three) styles of travel, depending on the nature and duration of your journey.

Travel Agency

Trekking and expedition agencies based in your home country exist to take care of every part of your trip. These companies secure international flights, arrange internal transport, book hotels, offer appropriate insurance, arrange permits and hire guides. A responsible agency will also help you obtain a visa, place you in a group of people with a similar level of mountain experience to your own, and offer advice on suitable types of clothing and equipment. An agency can also act as an emergency point of contact for your relatives whilst you are in-country. In the event that you have a less-than-satisfactory experience, the travel agency is likely to be accountable to the laws of your own country. Of course, this level of service comes at a certain price, which is why booking through a travel agency is normally more expensive than using an in-country operator.

In-Country Operator

The majority of travel agencies use in-country operators. Some of these companies are wholly or partly owned by the relevant agency, whilst others are independent businesses which sell their services to one or more agencies (or other in-country operators). Booking directly with an in-country operator cuts out the middle-man (in this case the travel agency) and is therefore cheaper; sometimes by a significant amount. There are various ways to track down a suitable company: you might receive a personal recommendation by someone who has travelled with a particular outfit, or decide to take the advice of a recently published guidebook or magazine article. Most people who book with an in-country operator have time on their side and are able to personally visit the various businesses upon arrival. Booking directly with an in-country operator is not always the ideal solution for backpackers who have only a short period of time at their disposal and no prior experience of their intended destination. Bear in mind that if you do receive a poor service, obtaining any sort of compensation in certain countries could be a forlorn hope.

One significant advantage of in-country operators is that most will be prepared to make partial arrangements for you. For example, you might ask the operator to only organise internal flights and trekking permits. Or you might want to hire a guide, but choose to carry all your own personal equipment rather than employing additional porters or pack animals.

Allow sufficient time to obtain the correct visa and permits

QUESTIONS TO ASK YOUR TRAVEL AGENCY OR IN-COUNTRY OPERATOR

In order to decide which company is most likely to offer the service that you require, you might want to raise some of the following issues before parting with any cash:

- Is the money that you pay held in a trust until your return, or is the company bonded to an organisation that protects your money? In the event that the company runs into financial difficulty – or should you make a claim for compensation – a bond or trust will increase the chance of a full or partial refund.

- What training has the leader of your trip received? What relevant experience does he have? Does he speak your language or do you speak his? It is essential that leaders of trips above 2500m have an understanding of the risks posed by altitude-related illnesses.

- What arrangements (including communications) are in place for an evacuation of a client or member of staff in the event of an emergency? Will you be expected to pay up-front for a rescue, or will the operator liaise with your insurance company on your behalf?

- Are all staff (including porters) adequately clothed, equipped and insured?

- What is the minimum group size, and how soon before departure might the company cancel the trip if there are insufficient clients?

- What is the maximum group size, and does the company guarantee that additional clients will not be attached to the party at the last minute?

- Does the company feel that it has a responsibility to protect the environment? Do they have a written environmental policy? Do they adhere to it? Can you see a copy of it?

- Can you visit the company's offices to discuss the trip with a member of staff before parting with any money?

Reputable companies will always be happy to answer these and any other questions that you might have.

There are thousands of unclimbed peaks left in the world: all but one of the mountains in this photograph await a first ascent

Going It Alone

Going it alone can create a wonderful sense of independence. You are answerable to no-one and, unlike on trips organised by travel agencies, you are not required to make any effort to be sociable with people in a group who are simply 'not your type'. You are more likely to be accepted by local communities than if you travel with several other people. You can take as many days off as your schedule will allow and alter your itinerary on a whim. However, should things start to go askew, you will have no-one to turn to for advice and assistance; in an emergency you will probably have to rely entirely on the sympathy of complete strangers. It is also important to point out that there are certain mountain regions in the world where trekking on your own is inadvisable because of the political situation in the country. *Appendix A includes a list of organisations able to identify destinations unsuitable for solo travel.*

Of course, there is a way to deflect some of these potential drawbacks, and that is to travel independently with a friend (or friends). There is at least a modicum of psychological strength to draw on when your team numbers more than one, albeit at the expense of uninhibited freedom.

If you choose to travel independently (either on your own or with friends) you will need to take on all the tasks that would otherwise have been handled by a company. Securing visas, registering with your embassy and organising communication with the outside world in an emergency are just some of the many logistics you will need to concern yourself with.

In addition to a visa, you may need a permit to trek in a particular region or to climb a certain mountain. Such requests are usually processed by the government's ministry of tourism, or the country's official mountaineering body. These permits might take a long time to secure, so as soon as you have decided where you want to go, it is a good idea to contact the embassy and find out whether such permissions are required. Indeed, government regulations may require you to enlist the services of an in-country operator. *Appendix A includes the contact details for the embassies and mountaineering associations of countries popular with climbers and trekkers.*

Other trekking permits can only be obtained when you arrive in-country. It is worth arriving early at the department that issues the permits, in order to avoid the inevitable mid-morning queues. Find out in advance the cost of the permit, and in what denomination payment is required. Try to have the exact money. If you cannot be bothered to stand in line, then find an in-country agent who is prepared to arrange your permit in return for a small fee.

If you do choose to go it alone, build in sufficient time to organise all the necessary paperwork. It is probably worth keeping a couple of spare self-portraits in your passport whilst travelling, just in case one is required to accompany an unexpected piece of documentation. It is advisable to carry photocopies of all your essential documents.

If you are buying tickets for an internal flight into the mountains, double-check that the ticket is for a confirmed seat and not 'request-only'. A request-only seat merely places you on a waiting list. Given the unpredictability of some mountain flights, you could be in for a long wait; delays of 10 days and more for people with request-only tickets are not that uncommon. The weight limit for baggage on internal flights – particularly in light aircraft and aeroplanes flying at high altitude – might be less than that permitted on international flights. The weight allowance on these flights is normally rigorously enforced.

In good weather, light aircraft can provide fast access to many mountains

Although there is usually no need to re-confirm your international outward flight, it is essential that you always re-confirm any onward and return flights a minimum of 72 hours before departure. Whilst people on an organised trip will normally have this taken care of by their travel agency, if you are travelling independently and are planning to return to the city less than three days before your flight home, you might need to leave your ticket with an in-country travel agent (who for a small fee will re-confirm your ticket whilst you are away). Or you can re-confirm the flight with the airline on arrival, before you set out on your trek or climb.

STILL UNDECIDED?

If you are unable to decide whether to sign up with a commercial company or sort everything out yourself, don't worry. The following chapters and appendices will guide you through all the considerations you will need to take into account when planning your adventure in the mountains. By learning more about what is involved, you will be in a better position to decide whether the complete package, a partial service or total independence is the most suitable approach for you. But before all of that, let's have a look in the next chapter at what a day in the mountain involves.

YOUR QUESTIONS ANSWERED

I've checked out the guidebooks but I can't find any information on the trek that I want to do. Where else can I go for advice?

Whilst many general guidebooks to individual countries give an overall impression of various mountain regions, they often have only limited space to describe individual treks. There is a fairly good chance that a dedicated trekking guide exists to the place that you want to visit. If your local bookstore or outdoor shop cannot help, contact a book distributor or publisher directly (many have up-to-date websites). A useful point of contact is the British Mountaineering Council (BMC) Information Service, which holds fact sheets on 130 countries including such esoteric destinations as the Cayman Islands, Jamaica and Vietnam. All of these are freely available to BMC members. The Information Service also has booklets on popular destinations for mountain travellers including East Africa, India, Nepal and South America. *For more details about the BMC Information Service, see Appendix F. Contact details for specialist book distributors and retailers can be found in Appendix A.*

2

> *Take Sherpa-size steps and even the steepest pass will not be a daunting prospect.*

Garry Weare

The Mountain Day

Whilst every mountain region has its own idiosyncrasies, painting a broad brush-stroke picture of what to expect during a typical day in the mountains might serve to relieve some of the natural anxieties felt by many people before their first camping or lodge-based trek.

UP AND ABOUT

The mountain day normally gets off to an early start in order to take advantage of comfortable trekking temperatures in the first part of the morning. If you are travelling with an organised party, your cook team is likely to stir well before first light to prepare 'bed tea' and bowls of hot washing water. After you have packed up your belongings, non-cooking staff will strike your tent and prepare the loads for the day: it is quite normal to see your bag disappearing up the trail on the back of a porter or pack animal whilst you are still eating breakfast. As soon as you have finished your meal and filled up your water bottle, you can get underway.

This routine, pioneered in Nepal, is spreading with varying success to other parts of the world. For example, on Kilimanjaro, reputable companies are now endeavouring to provide a similar service (although some of the staff who work on Africa's highest mountain have had considerably less time to perfect their operations than the Sherpas). Elsewhere, the concept of client care might be totally lost on your staff and you could well be expected to play an equal part in preparing breakfast, dismantling tents and packing up equipment.

If you are staying in a tea house or hostel, then it is worth bearing in mind that it might take the owner quite a while to get the stove going. Rather than waiting for breakfast, a faster start to the day can often be achieved by paying your bill the night before and skipping out the door at around 7am. A packet of biscuits and a bottle of boiled water (purchased during the evening) will probably be sufficient to keep you going until mid-morning, at which point you can dive into another tea house for a quick breakfast. People who choose to camp independently may find that it takes up to two hours to strike camp and hit the trail.

TRAVEL AT ALTITUDE

At altitude, mountaineers and trekkers will need to choose the optimum time of day to get up and about. This will depend on a number of factors including:

- The ambient and windchill temperature
- The number of daylight hours available
- The distance to be travelled
- The amount of equipment that needs to be carried
- The conditions underfoot

In light of all these factors, people heading to altitude for the first time may want to be modest in their ambitions.

Sometimes a pre-dawn start will help you to maximise the chance of reaching the next camp whilst the ice is still firm underfoot and before the sunshine envelops you.

> " I like to make an early start in order to get the bulk of the day's journey done by midday. If you start late, you end up worrying about being overtaken by darkness. "
>
> *Tim Salmon*

ON THE TRAIL

It can often be quite cold when you set out in the morning. People begin the day either by wearing just a couple of layers (and endure the first few chilly minutes before their internal heating systems kick in) or else bundle themselves up in most of their clothes for the first ten minutes before stopping to adjust their attire.

In many mountain regions, the accuracy of available maps might require careful interpretation

If you opt to use a water bottle equipped with a flexible hose attachment, and fill your pockets with snacks, then you will be able to maintain energy levels throughout the day without having to stop just to eat and drink. *You can read more about water and nutrition in Chapter 9.*

The secret of success with trekking is (weather permitting) to get the larger part of the day's route completed by lunchtime. Starting early allows for the maximum amount of daylight to deal with problems resulting from exhaustion, illness or injury. For example, if you find the way ahead barred by rockfall or a landslide, additional daylight hours might save the party from becoming benighted. Experienced backpackers always carry a headtorch in their daysacks, just in case darkness overtakes them. If you decide to do likewise, it is worth disconnecting the battery during the day.

CONSERVING ENERGY

The way that you move has a great bearing on the number of calories that you burn up. Inexperienced 'hares' often stride out and attempt to reach the first pass ahead of everyone else. Wiser 'tortoises' move at a more leisurely pace that they can maintain for several hours, thus ensuring that they do not run out of energy before the end of the day. Tucking hands into pockets, or

Depending on the trek you choose, you might encounter anything from lush pastures...

❝Almost everyone neglects to drink enough. A serious lack of inclination to drink can be misinterpreted as an instruction from the body not to drink. Plain water is boring but flavouring works wonders. Adding some electrolytes on really long or hot days can also make a big difference.❞

Henry Todd

around shoulder straps, can save a surprising amount of energy. By contrast, trekking pole advocates claim that using two poles is an effective way to reduce overall fatigue. Certainly, trekking poles can make all the difference on unstable terrain. Heavy boots can also burn up oodles of calories. The ideal footwear will be light in weight and provide sufficient protection for the feet and ankles on the type of terrain you expect to encounter.

BREAKING FOR LUNCH

Your schedule – and the weather – will often heavily influence any decision about whether or not to stop for lunch. If you are trekking in hot conditions (and mountains can become ferociously hot) then an ultra-early

start, followed by an extended lunchbreak in the shade to avoid the sun as it reaches its zenith, will spare you from walking in the energy-sapping heat of the middle part of the day. Conversely, foul weather is often encouragement enough to keep everyone going, albeit at a slightly slower pace.

If you do stop for lunch, try to resist the temptation to simply flake out. There are lots of little jobs that you can do whilst eating which are better done in the warmth of the day than in the cool of the evening. Why not take your boots off? This will give your socks a chance to dry out, and allow you to check your feet for blisters. You could also get your sleeping bag out. The body releases a surprisingly large amount of perspiration every night, most of which passes through your bag. However, some moisture is

6For your first high altitude expedition try an easier 6000er to begin with. If you handle the altitude well – and most importantly enjoy the experience – try a few harder ones before moving on to the higher peaks.9

Tim Macartney-Snape

inevitably retained in the wadding. After a few nights without an airing, your sleeping bag will begin to lose some of its insulating qualities. Spreading your bag out at lunch will help to improve its efficiency. Lunchtime also provides an opportunity to attend to any running repairs of your clothing and equipment.

HOW FAR TO GO?

Unlike in the UK, where the distance that remains to be covered is measured in kilometres or miles, it is quite usual for people who live in some mountain regions to describe distances in hours and minutes. Although you might question the validity of this – after all, who is to say that everyone walks at the same pace? – in reality the hours quoted in popular trekking regions are usually 'tourist' hours. Many local people are capable of covering the same ground in half the time it takes the trekker. Of course, if you are trekking at altitude, then the critical aspect of the day will not be time or distance but the height gained: above 2500m, the rule of thumb is to sleep no more than 300m higher than the previous night and to take a rest day every third day. *You can read all about the effects of altitude in Chapter 10.*

ARRIVING AT CAMP

If your day has gone well then you will probably roll into camp sometime between 3pm and 5pm. Replacing your damp shirt with a dry one as soon as you arrive is a quick way to start feeling warm and comfortable.

If you are trekking with a group, the rest of the afternoon is now yours to do with as you please. You might want to get stuck in with pitching the tents alongside your staff or go for a walk to a local village or viewpoint. It is courteous to inform your guide if you do go for a stroll to prevent a search party being mustered unnecessarily. On the other hand, a drink of water and a snooze could be in order if you are suffering a little from the altitude. Dinner is usually served around 7pm. Unless there is plenty of tea on the table, and you are feeling particularly sociable, it is quite normal to retire immediately after supper. If you do stay up, bear in mind that the dining tent might double up as the sleeping tent for your porters.

If you are tea house trekking, it is a smart move to order your evening meal early. For whilst there might be a great variety of dishes on the menu, it is likely that there will be only one stove and only one cook.

If you are camping without guides and staff then the responsibility for finding a safe campsite, firing up the stove and cooking your evening meal will rest squarely on your shoulders. However, it is this level of self-sufficiency that attracts some people to the outdoor life. *Cooking procedures are described in Chapter 9; guidelines for choosing a campsite can be found in Chapter 3.*

LIGHTS OUT

When you do retire for the evening take care to ensure that your pee bottle, headtorch, water bottle, toilet paper, medical kit and boots are to hand, in case you start to feel ill, want a drink or need to visit the toilet in the middle of the night.

YOUR QUESTIONS ANSWERED

Do I need a map and compass?

Hillwalkers familiar with navigating their way around British mountains using map and compass - and who then go trekking along popular trails abroad for the first time - are often surprised at just how straightforward navigation on certain routes is. Many famous trails are established paths used by local villagers, making a map and compass virtually redundant. Of course, this is no excuse for not learning how to use a compass properly, especially when you are in a remote area (or experience poor visibility) and are in possession of a detailed map. However, in many places the accuracy of available maps is woeful. Some are no more than crude outlines of peaks, passes and villages, and even these features might be marked in the wrong places. Whilst a Global Positioning System (GPS) receiver would be able to inform you of your current position, this could prove to be of little use if the map you are using is inaccurate. Military maps are normally drawn to a high standard, although getting hold of these can often be difficult, expensive and even illegal.

Throughout the day, you will probably want to remember key features that you come across in case you are forced to retreat. One way to do this is to annotate your map or guidebook as you go along. Some routes are marked with symbols painted on boulders and trees. However, the same logo might be used to mark more than one trail, so take care at junctions. *GPS is described in Chapter 14, whilst Appendix A includes details of companies who are able to supply hard-to-find maps. There are several excellent books dedicated to the instruction of map and compass; some of these are listed in Appendix E.*

3

> ❝If you leave a camp or snowhole unattended, make sure that it is well secured and well marked. It requires a huge effort to carry all the gear and supplies up there and they may be irreplaceable. You don't want to sweat all the way back up to a camp to find that it is buried and gone forever.❞

Stephen Venables

A Place To Stay

Whether you are camping or staying in lodges, finding somewhere to stay each night can occupy several daylight hours.

HOSTELS AND HUTS

People travelling without tents are likely to discover that as they move further into the mountains, buildings become scarcer and more simple (both in construction and in the facilities they offer). Some hostels might offer private rooms as well as

Tea houses promise all sorts of delights...

dormitory accommodation, but in all cases it is wise to bring your own toilet paper, as well as a towel and flip flops for the shower. By contrast, mountain huts might be equipped with little more than wooden bunk beds and a place to light up your stove. Unless you are staying in a hut that you know has a resident guardian and shared cooking facilities, it is best to arrive with everything that you need, including food. Bed bugs are a problem in some types of accommodation; a sleeping bag liner will help to minimise the chance of being bitten.

FIRE AND SECURITY

Regardless of the type of building that you stay in, take a few moments to consider the fire and security aspects of the construction. It may prove impossible to retreat down a wooden staircase in the event of a blaze so perhaps a room on the ground floor would be more appropriate? On the other hand, a ground floor apartment is easier for a thief to break into than a first floor bunkroom. Check any marked fire exits to ensure that they are not locked or bolted. Other questions to answer include:

• Are there any fire extinguishers and do you know how to operate them?
• Is there a no smoking rule and is it enforced?
• How is the door to your room secured and does it have a padlock?

Take care to ensure that all candles are extinguished properly before turning in and make sure that naked flames are never left unattended.

ORGANISED CAMPING

The facilities on an organised campsite may range from covered ablutions, laundry facilities, entertainment for children, and an on-site shop through to just a field (with or without a tap). The country that you visit does not necessarily determine the grade of organised site you are likely to find: for instance, many types are available throughout the European Alps.

Organised campsites are normally found in sheltered valleys that can be easily reached by road. They can be useful places to find a trekking or climbing partner. However, some sites have a restriction on the size of the party and most have 'quiet hours' after 10 or 11pm. If you choose to camp, make every effort to seek permission from – and pay a fair price to – the landowner. Booking ahead is advisable during peak periods in popular locations.

WILD CAMPING

Travelling with a tent and sleeping bag allows you to camp wherever you
want, providing that you are not breaking any laws of trespass. With a tent,
you can stay to watch the sunset long after the last hut-based trekkers have
retired for the night and the final backpackers have trooped off to their
organised campsite. Camping in a remote location is close to the sharp end
of the accommodation scale. The decision to experience wild camping is
not one to be taken lightly; there are several factors to take into account, as
well as the responsibility to ensure that the site you choose is left in a
pristine condition upon your departure.

CHOOSING A PLACE TO CAMP

By finding a suitable place to camp earlier rather than later in the day, you
will have plenty of time to complete all your tasks – from erecting the tent
to cooking your meal – during daylight hours. Ideally, the site you
plump for will be near enough to a water source to make collection for
cooking and drinking easy but not so close that you are plagued by insects,
kept awake by the sound of running water or washed away during a flash
flood: that comfortable bed of sand in a dry watercourse can quickly
become a raging torrent. Don't forget to look above your head. Are there
any pylons or trees that could blow down in a gale? Is there a danger of
rockfall or avalanche? Have you stopped in a clearing that is an emergency
helicopter landing pad? What angle is the ground lying at? Perfectly level
ground might make for a comfortable night's sleep, but rainwater will have
nowhere to drain to. In a downpour, this could lead to a waterlogged tent.
By contrast, a gentle slope will encourage surface water to drain away.

> When on a
> popular
> trekking trail
> lined with tea
> houses, I
> carry my own
> mug, to buy hot
> drinks
> directly from
> the pot rather
> than risk
> drinking out
> of a glass
> which has
> almost
> certainly not
> been washed
> properly. This
> helps to
> reduce the
> risk of
> infection.
>
> *George Band*

PITCHING YOUR TENT

Is the terrain covered in stones that might puncture the tent groundsheet? If you do move them away, will an obvious impression of the groundsheet be left in the soil, scarring the landscape and spoiling the wild camping experience for others? If you plan to camp in the same place for more than one week, re-pitching the tent in a slightly different location every few days might help to minimise the impact you make on the local environment. If you have no choice but to move stones, take the time to return them to their original positions before you move on. *You can read more about good environmental practice in Chapter 8.*

If the terrain refuses to accept plastic or metal pegs and there are no rocks to hand, there are a number of ways to secure your tent. Anchors can be produced by filling empty stuff sacks with sand or snow. These can then be tied to the tent's guylines and buried. If you find yourself on frozen turf or ice then ice axes and some types of climbing ironmongery can often be driven into the surface and used as tent anchors.

Positioning the main (or only) tent entrance out of the wind will prevent the inside of your ark taking on the appearance of a wind tunnel every time the front door is opened in bad weather. As soon as the tent is up, take a moment to secure the tent, pole and peg bags to one of the tent poles. That way you will be able to easily find them in the morning.

One effective camp procedure is to have a 'clean' and a 'dirty' side to the site. All toilet, washing and rubbish collection facilities are located in the dirty area. Waste water can also be poured away on the dirty side, allowing drinking water to be collected from the clean area.

SNOWHOLES AND SHOVEL-UPS

In the right conditions, snow can be a wonderful building material. If proof of this was ever needed, just look at the marvellous igloos perfected by the Inuits. On a windswept plateau it might prove possible to cut blocks out of the snow and then pile them up on one or more sides of your tent in order to create a windbreak. For added protection, the tent can be pitched in the crater you have dug.

Another option (which dispenses of the tent altogether) is the 'shovel-up'. Snow is heaped into a pile with a shovel (the larger the blade, the better) and allowed to consolidate. The inside is then excavated and piled on the outside. This process of consolidation, excavation and piling can continue ad infinitum until you have created a dome large enough for the entire group.

Allow plenty of time to dig a snowhole

A third type of snow shelter is the snowhole. In sub-zero conditions, a snowhole can provide a virtually indestructible refuge. Creating a snowhole is hard work (assume at least one hour of digging for a one-person hole and a subsequent hour for each additional person who needs to be accommodated). Over a period of several days the snowhole will shrink and it may be necessary to carve out more living space. Don't forget to burn a candle whilst you are in the hole. If it snuffs itself out then immediately open the tunnel entrance or poke a ski pole through the roof to increase the amount of oxygen in your snowhole.

PLANNED BIVOUACS

A bivouac is essentially a night out using a temporary shelter other than a tent. Traditionally, a bivouac consisted of a waterproof tarp tied to a rock or tree and set at an angle to minimise water ingress. More recently, tarps have been augmented – and in many instances replaced – by bivouac or 'bivi' bags. These are sleeping bag sheaths made from waterproof/breathable fabrics. *You can read more about bivi bags in Chapter 13.*

The advantages and disadvantages of bivi equipment over a tent are clear. A bivi is lighter and takes up less space than a tent, both on the ground and in your rucksack. If you do not plan to camp on a regular basis, carrying a bivi bag can be excellent insurance against being 'caught out'. A bivi also allows one to watch the stars and to literally get closer to nature. However, in mosquito-infested locations, such closeness might prove to be a disadvantage. Unless you can find an overhang to shelter under, relying solely on a bivi bag can be a miserable experience in prolonged wet weather. Nevertheless, it is worth bearing in mind that the chance of a tent being blown away in a gale is often higher than a person lying prone in a bivi bag.

> In wet places – such as the Ruwenzori – always keep one dry set of clothes in a stout polythene bag. Then, however soaked and miserable you get during the day, you can always be warm and comfortable at night.
>
> *Stephen Venables*

Preparing for a bivouac in the last light of the day

ENFORCED BIVOUACS

An enforced bivouac (brought on perhaps by benightment or injury) without any camping or bivi gear is a serious proposition. If you are able to lose height safely, give serious thought to doing so: the ambient temperature will increase by 1°C for every 150m that you descend. Is there any sort of shelter around? Finding somewhere out of the wind and rain will greatly improve your situation.

Your overall predicament can be made less grave by always carrying an inexpensive 'survival' bag. If you succeed in finding some form of cover that protects you from the elements, then you can get into the survival bag as you would a sleeping bag. In wet or exposed conditions, a survival bag is best employed by tearing one corner off to create a breathing hole. Next, pull the bag over your head and sit down on your rucksack with the excess plastic pulled under your bottom. By morning the survival bag will probably be running with sweat, but you should have at least survived the night. People trekking in a group can swap their individual survival bags for a lightweight frameless tent (known as a 'bothy bag' or 'zdarski sack') that allows all members to shelter together.

If you set out without a survival bag and are unable to find any sort of effective shelter, then prepare yourself for a rough night – even if the weather is calm. To improve the situation, wear all your spare clothing, waterproofs, hat and gloves. Feet and legs can be put into an empty rucksack. Do everything you can to insulate yourself from the ground. Does your rucksack have a removable foam backpad that can be used as a seat? If you are in a group, crowding together is warmer than sitting separately. Huddling also allows you to talk the night away, and easily share food and drink.

No matter how grim the situation is that you find yourself in, you might draw some comfort from remembering that it is 'only' one night and that your surroundings will look somewhat cheerier in the morning. Do not underestimate the physical toll that an enforced night out has on the body. Most people choose to retreat at first light after a night out in the open.

YOUR QUESTIONS ANSWERED

I can't decide whether to backpack independently and stay in lodges, or join an organised camping trek. What are the differences and what facilities can I expect to find in a mountain lodge?

A lodge or tea house is akin to a basic hostel, with dormitories and/or private rooms. A sleeping bag is usually required. If you are confident that the route you are following is liberally dotted with lodges, you will not have to pack cooking gear or a tent.

On an organised camping trek, the company may supply mattresses and sleeping bags. If they do, it's worth taking your own sleeping bag liner along, and maybe a mat too as the type often provided squashes down to nothing when sat upon. A trekking operator will also supply guides, a cook team, dining and toilet tents, as well as porters or pack animals to transport the majority of your gear.

If you stay in tea houses, you will be responsible for carrying all your own equipment, unless you choose to hire a porter in each village for the following day. Bear in mind that if you do this you will be morally obliged to look after your employee. The chance of him having personal insurance is almost zero. By comparison, a reputable trekking agency will insure its staff against injury.

If you trek independently, you will also need to sort out your own trekking permits. Permits for some regions are not required (although an environmental permit may need to be obtained). You need to allow time in your schedule to obtain any necesssary permits. Certain areas can only be visited if you are with an organised group.

If you like the idea of tea house trekking but don't want to carry your own gear, several operators now offer tea house treks. *You can read more about hiring staff in Chapter 4.*

> *Treat your local staff - guides, cooks and porters - like members of your team. If they feel appreciated, they will work harder for you and your trip will be a happier one.*
>
> *Steve Bell*

Are all your porters properly clothed and equipped?

Local People

Few parties are able to remain entirely self sufficient for very long in mountainous regions. So unless you are heading off to a mountain region that is devoid of any human habitation (and there are fewer of these than you might think) then some interaction with the local populace is almost inevitable.

STAFF WELFARE

All tourists have a moral responsibility to ensure that the staff they employ (either directly, or indirectly via a travel agency) are looked after. Whilst regular staff such as guides and cooks are often properly clothed and equipped by the travel agency, village porters employed on a casual basis are frequently left to sort themselves out. Porters usually have the right equipment to survive below the treeline. But above this height they require additional clothing and shelter.

It can be all-too-easy to ignore a porter's complaints: local people casually employed by treks and expeditions who are not able to pull their weight or who become sick are sometimes dismissed and sent home alone, as the following tragic story illustrates.

> *In bad conditions, my porters share my tent.*
>
> *Smiler Cuthbertson*

"On October 24th 1997, a 24-year old Nepalese mountain porter, Shyam Bahdur Nepali, fell ill whilst carrying a commercial trekking company's equipment over the Thorong La, a 5200 metre pass on the Annapurna Circuit. Unable to carry his load, he was paid off, dismissed from the trek and sent back alone without adequate clothing for the cold conditions. He managed to stagger down to 4200m and spent the night alone in a half-built lodge where he was given a blanket and food by the local owner. The next morning he collapsed. No treatment was given to him until late that afternoon when an American climber arrived and was asked to take a look at him. Shyam was diagnosed as suffering from severe High Altitude Pulmonary Oedema and High Altitude Cerebral Oedema. Shyam was given the correct medicine as well as gloves, a hat, a blanket and a torch. £30 was raised to employ two porters to carry Shyam down that night to the Himalayan Rescue Association (HRA) aid post in Manang. Unfortunately, treacherous conditions forced the porters to descend slowly and Shyam died that night, just one hour away from the rescue station. His body lay by the trail for three days."

Porters are the lifeblood of treks and expeditions in the Himalaya

In response to the death of Shyam and other porters, the eminent mountain doctor Jim Duff has set up the International Porter Protection Group (IPPG), which actively campaigns for the rights of local people. Whilst some people insist that it is the duty of each trekking operator to make sure its staff are properly cared for, the owners of some companies are unscrupulous, and will do anything to make a quick profit. In reality, it is the individual tourist who holds the magic wand: we can choose to travel only with organisations that look after their staff. Some of the questions you might want to ask your trekking operator include:

- Is every member of staff adequately clothed and equipped?
- Are there a sufficient number of staff available to accompany a sick person (porter or client) down in the event of illness?
- Has the company received any third-party awards or endorsements as a result of its staffing policies?

If every tourist were to ask these questions before paying a deposit for their 'holiday of a lifetime' then the entire industry would be forced to change overnight. However, costs would rise. What financial price are we prepared to pay in order to help protect the lives of the people who labour long and hard under monstrous loads for us?

Utilising the services of a company that does ensure the safety of its staff is good news for the porter and the client: an employee who is properly fed, clothed and insured, and who knows that he will receive the best available medical treatment if he is injured, is more likely to go out of his way to assist his clients as he will be worrying less about his own situation.

INTERNATIONAL PORTER PROTECTION GROUP GUIDELINES

The aim of the IPPG is to improve the health and safety of the trekking porter and reduce the incidence of avoidable illness, injury and death. The IPPG does this by raising awareness of the issue among trekking and travel companies, leaders, head porters and trekkers. The organisation recommends that:

- Sufficient clothing be available for protection in bad weather and at altitude. This should include adequate footwear, hat, gloves, sunglasses and windproofs, as well as access to a blanket and sleeping mat above the snowline.
- Leaders and trekkers should provide the same standard of medical care for porters as they have for themselves.
- Porters should not be paid off because of illness without the leader or trekkers being informed.
- Sick porters never be sent down alone, but with someone who speaks their language and understands the problem.
- Sufficient funds must be provided to rescue and treat sick porters.

If you are going to a remote area, try to select strong and experienced porters. High altitude and remote treks require correspondingly high-grade clothing and equipment to be issued. Contact details for the International Porter Protection Group can be found in Appendix A.

LODGE-BASED AND CAMPING TREKS

Many mountain lodge and tea house aficionados believe that by trekking independently and using local accommodation they are putting hard cash in the hands of the people who need it most. Whilst this may be true, it doesn't necessarily mean that all commercial companies are fleecing their staff. Reputable operators employ their guides and cooks year-round, even when there is no work (such as during the monsoon season). Furthermore, they provide for the family of an employee if he suffers an accident and is unable to work. It is worth remembering that on a typical organised trek for 10 tourists, up to 30 local people may be employed. Hiring local people is an effective way to distribute cash to poor areas away from the main trails, where many of the porters come from.

Trekkers who carry their own gear and stay in lodges employ no-one, but do use facilities provided by local families. Whilst trekking without staff can be quite liberating, it is ironic that certain wild areas are becoming increasingly urbanised in destinations where lodges are flourishing.

CULTURAL CONSIDERATIONS

Whilst a book of this length cannot do justice to the very many cultural differences to be found in mountain regions around the world, certain points apply to most areas and religions.

The trekker or climber visiting a country for the first time cannot help but make a cultural *faux pas* or two, but local people who recognise that you are attempting to respect their way of life will often be most forgiving. It is worth remembering that visitors who show an interest in regional customs often encourage a sense of pride amongst local people, and this often goes a long way to ensure that your visit does not contribute to the demise of traditions. As a result of your attitude, you may be invited to gain an insight into family life and other rites that less sensitive tourists are not permitted to see. At the same time, you might have the opportunity to put across a more realistic view of the way of life in your own country than the stereotypic image often portrayed through advertising and the media.

Some guidebooks include information about local customs. Indeed, there is now at least one range of books dedicated to describing the cultures of individual countries. Learning a little about the language, history and current affairs of the nation and the local area may go a long way to removing some of the frustrations you might otherwise experience.

> ❛Try and learn at least a few words of the local language. If nothing else you will give the porters a few easy laughs.❜
>
> *Jon Tinker*

Simply observing the actions of local people will often provide you with answers on what to do if approached by beggars, what to wear in a temple, or whether shoes should be removed before entering the home. Bear in mind that in some countries, tea and small talk always precede negotiation no matter how urgent the situation is. By absorbing aspects of the culture and social etiquette you will do much to endear yourself to the local people.

In many countries, skimpy or tight-fitting clothing is frowned upon, as are overt and public displays of affection. Both hands, or the right hand only, is often used to give and receive food, as the left hand is viewed by some societies as being ritually and physically 'unclean'. Some religions forbid their devotees to eat food that has been touched by another person, so only accept onto your plate what you know you can eat. Gifts – including money – may be exchanged with both hands.

Photography

As with local customs, there is no hard and fast rule about taking photographs of local people. Whilst many individuals are only too happy to be photographed, others will go to great lengths to avoid being captured on film. Simply asking the subject before taking a photograph shows respect and may produce unexpected results; people have been known to bring out their entire families to be photographed. If you are reluctant to do this because of the formal pose that is often struck by people, why not shoot one frame and then another after everyone has relaxed? A Polaroid camera can be a massive boon in building friendly relations – but when word gets out about your gadget, expect to get through a lot of film. If you don't have a camera capable of producing an instant result, try to avoid agreeing to send copies of photos when you know that it will prove virtually impossible to honour such promises.

ADDITIONAL CONSIDERATIONS FOR GROUPS

People planning to hire their own staff rather than use the services of a commercial operator may find the following guidelines to be of practical benefit. Individuals interested in the work that reputable operators and trek leaders put in behind the scenes might also find these notes interesting.

Recruiting Your Staff

Where will you recruit your staff from? Confining employment to villagers who live at roadheads or near airstrips may cause resentment amongst local people who live in other settlements. Certain regions have a system of

> Remember porters – our supporters – are human beings with their own limitations and a different culture. They do this to earn money. Unlike us, very few do it for the fun of it.
>
> *Harish Kapadia*

'First to rise, last to bed'; a cook team smile their way through another long day

sharing out employment equally amongst a number of villages. In some countries, accredited porters will hold licences. If such a system exists in the country you are visiting, give due consideration to supporting it.

It can be very easy to hire the first local guide that you meet but perhaps it is better to wait a few hours to see who else turns up; word of your arrival is likely to spread very quickly. It is always worth seeking a personal recommendation for a guide and cook, either by word-of-mouth or from guidebooks. Some guides and porters carry letters of recommendation from previous clients. If you want to hire someone for just a few days on a provisional basis, make sure that there can be no misunderstanding about the terms of your employment. Keep in mind that very occasionally porters and guides loaded with expedition equipment have been known to disappear around a bend in the trail, never to be seen again.

If your working relationship with a local person starts to deteriorate for an unspecified reason, try to find out if something you have said or done has inadvertently caused offence. Sometimes it could be the case that a serious problem has developed. If your guide or head porter is unwilling to talk about it, you might be forced to ask the porters directly what the problem is. It is worth noting that body language as well as verbal comments can often have completely different meanings in different cultures. For example, you might feel annoyed if the prospective guide whom you are interviewing avoids all eye contact. Yet whilst this might strike you as the demeanour of a shifty and potentially dishonest character, in his culture making eye contact might be considered rude.

Agreeing Upon Fair Terms And Conditions

Try to find out from other people who have recently been to the region
what the going rate is for porters, guides and cooks. In some areas, wages
are laid down in writing by the local administration (although these may be
difficult to enforce on a wet and remote hillside that is several weeks from
the nearest town). When discussing wages, it is worth going to the trouble
of raising, discussing and agreeing the points described below. If possible,
have the contract written down in English and the local language. If none of
the porters can write, try and find a village representative who can.

The Daily Rate For An Agreed Load Or Job

How far will each day's march be? What weight will be carried? How many
rest days will be necessary? What payment will be made for bad weather
days that prevent movement? How many meals will the cook team provide
each day? Will the same team stick with the party for the entire duration, or
will new staff be hired as the expedition progresses? Bear in mind that some
local people may be reluctant to stray more than a couple of days from their
village, especially if they have crops or livestock to attend to. In this
instance, or if the trek is ending in a different place from where it begins,
how many days will it take for an unloaded member of staff to return home?
An unloaded porter may be able to make the return journey two or three
times faster than the outward leg, but he will expect to be paid for the
homeward trip. If you are heading to 'Base Camp' make sure that both
parties agree exactly where this is, or you could find your loads being
dropped several miles short of your planned camp.

When all of the points have been agreed upon, make sure that the
information is clearly communicated to all of the staff, but do not be
surprised if the head porter or guide takes a cut of each person's salary as
payment for conducting negotiations.

Food, Fuel, Equipment And Insurance

Some travellers pay their local staff a cash sum instead of providing food,
fuel, shelter and clothing. This is fine if the staff have adequate equipment,
and actually go and buy what provisions they do not have. However, in
many instances they will pocket the money, grit their teeth and prepare to
be cold, wet and hungry. In adverse or high altitude situations this attitude
can rebound on everyone if a member of staff requires medical treatment or
simply cannot go on as a result of inadequate clothing or food. So if you are
hiring people, you have an obligation to check that your staff really do
possess the correct equipment and supplies before setting out. Staff being

> The wage you
> pay for
> porters'
> services
> should be in
> line with
> local laws and
> customs.
> Tipping too
> much or paying
> more than the
> prevailing
> rate should be
> avoided.
> Otherwise you
> will spoil the
> individual and
> create a cheat
> for the
> future.
>
> *Harish Kapadia*

'Do unto others as you would have them do unto you': don't unwittingly become the ugly tourist by forgetting your manners.

Tim Macartney-Snape

employed to work on a mountaineering expedition will need to be clothed and equipped with gear similar to that being used by the expedition team. Some employees might already own satisfactory high altitude gear, in which case a cash payment might be more appropriate.

Sufficient stoves and fuel will allow the porters to drink and eat enough hot water and food, and may provide an alternative to the traditional (but environmentally unsustainable) wood fire. In some areas, dried dung can be used as a fuel on fires that are started with only a small amount of wood. Mess tents provide rudimentary protection for porters at night.

If you need to supply certain items that the porters do not have – such as sunglasses – think carefully about the best time to distribute them. For example, if you know that you will be encountering a snowy pass, you might want to hand the glasses out on the day of the crossing. This will prevent anyone from selling or accidentally breaking their new shades before they arrive at the pass. Even then you might be faced with a battle of wills to get the staff to actually wear the sunglasses. A small stock of certain items (sunglasses, jackets and shoes) can come in very handy if one or two members of staff lose or forget to bring certain items of equipment with them. An organisation called Porters' Progress has opened clothing banks in Kathmandu and in the Everest region of Nepal. These banks work on a no-cost deposit system. The organisation is planning to open more banks in Nepal and in other mountain regions around the world, such as Kilimanjaro in Africa.

In some countries, insuring a local person may prove to be almost impossible. Think about soliciting advice from a person who has been to the area before. Some expeditions have found that they have been left with no choice but to hire staff through an in-country operator in order that insurance can be guaranteed. If you do this, ask to see a copy of the insurance policy. If an uninsured porter is killed or injured whilst in your care, you might feel a moral responsibility to take care of his family if the country you are in has no welfare state.

Expeditions need to ensure that all porters are able to deal with any technical ground that may need to be crossed. In this type of situation, it is standard practice to fix rope handrails, especially when ascending and descending tricky ground.

Packing The Loads To Be Carried

Loads need to be prepared with the assistance of your staff to ensure that they are comfortable and of the right size. For example, the pony men who work the route into Cerro Aconcagua in the Andes prefer wooden boxes to plastic barrels. Loads need to be of a similar weight, especially when they are being strapped to either side of an animal. It is always sensible to pack fuel away from other supplies. Make sure that kerosene is not carried near the skin of the porter or the hide of the animal, as this substance can cause irritation.

Using public transport is a great way to meet local people

A piece of plastic (from a local market) will prevent the load becoming soaked in a rainstorm. A better alternative is to put the load inside a kit bag and a waterproof liner. Locking the bag will put the porter carrying it beyond suspicion if an item goes missing. A spring balance will help to settle any disagreements about the weight being carried. If you have several loads, it might be worth taking the trouble to number all of them. Give some thought to implementing a tagging system to account for each load.

Whilst porters in a handful of mountain regions have earned a reputation for being unco-operative, the vast majority of local people are cheerful, hard-working and attentive to the needs of their clients. By remaining patient, polite and friendly at all times, by trying to entertain and encourage them during the day, and most importantly of all by treating them as equal members of your team, you will stand a good chance of building a strong and healthy working relationship with your porters: a relationship which will pay dividends if (and usually when) the going gets tough.

YOUR QUESTIONS ANSWERED

How much should I tip my porter?

In many mountain regions tipping is expected, and porters will want to know what tip they are going to receive even before they set out. This can prove frustrating as historically tips were only handed out for good service. One solution is to agree on the tip at the start of the trek, but make it clear that this will only be paid if good service is received. Incidents of poor service need to be pointed out when they occur, in order to give the staff the opportunity to put things right. It is impossible to say precisely what an appropriate tip might be as this varies from region to region, but one rule of thumb is to budget for an extra day's wage for a two or three week trek. It can be a good idea for all tips to be handed out publicly to each individual member of your staff so that each person knows what everyone else has received. In some mountain communities, equipment in lieu of cash is not acceptable, though of course gear may be presented to individual members of staff as a gift in addition to their tip.

> *Lodges and tea houses can be cosy places but they can also be bad places to pick up gastro-intestinal or respiratory bugs from fellow travellers. When eating, ensure that your plates and cutlery have been completely dried as the water used to wash them could be contaminated.*

Tim Macartney-Snape

Medical Matters

Medical considerations often come last on many people's pre-departure 'to-do' lists. After all, it can be all too easy to assume that the annual insurance policy bought last year for the family holiday will suffice, that an embassy official will somehow find out that you are in trouble and despatch a helicopter, and that the trek leader is sufficiently experienced in remote medical care. It is only when things start to go awry that these assumptions can turn out to be false.

After taking advice, it is down to the individual to decide what level of medical precautions should be taken. The optimum time to start sorting things out is about three months before departure. If you have less time than this, almost everything suggested here can still be achieved, albeit at a less leisurely pace.

The following information (together with the information included in Chapters 10 and 14) is aimed at the adult lay person who does not expect to have immediate access to medical advice whilst on a trek or climb. It is meant as a guide to mountain-related medical issues only, and does not seek to cover every possible ailment or disease that a person can encounter on a visit to a foreign country. *Appendix A contains a list of dedicated medical books that have been written with the mountain traveller in mind.*

THINGS TO CONSIDER BEFORE DEPARTURE

You will probably be more confident in dealing with any medical situations that arise if you have been able to carry out some research on your destination. For example, you might want to find out which hospitals have the most modern facilities, and whether the country has a state-owned or private air rescue service. Some countries may not have any sort of rescue facility. *You can read about identifying and assessing risks in Chapters 6 and 12.*

Medical Training

It is a sad fact that the chance of keeping a seriously injured individual alive in a remote mountain environment for any length of time is low. However, knowing how to splint a leg, bandage a wound and put a patient in the recovery position are valuable skills to have, both in everyday life and in the mountain environment. It might be possible to persuade your employer to send you on a medical course as the skills you learn will almost certainly be of use in the workplace. Or you could sign up for a dedicated mountain first aid course at an outdoor centre. The actions taken in the first few moments after a serious accident often make the difference between life and death.

Insurance

An insurance policy is essential, even if you are travelling no further afield than Europe and are already in possession of an E111 form (available from post offices). This is because – unlike in the UK – most countries charge for search, rescue and medical facilities. You might be tempted to buy the cheap insurance policy offered to you when you purchase your airline ticket. However, it could be a 'high volume, low risk' policy. The term 'low risk' refers to the insurer: the policy might be spiked with a battery of exclusions to minimise the chance of the company having to pay out in the event of a claim. By contrast, specialist travel insurance policies that cover all manner of mountain activities might cost more, but at least you will set off secure in the knowledge that you are not going to be refused help when you need it most. Before parting with any cash, why not ask for a copy of the insurance policy? Take particular note of any exclusions ('roped climbing' and 'off-piste skiing' are two popular phrases that many so-called travel insurance policies exclude) and whether they apply to your situation. Other things to consider include:

- Restrictions: on age, altitude, individual countries and virgin territory.
- Baggage: how much is the excess, and is it a new for old policy?
- Medical cover: the Consumer Association recommends a minimum of £1 million per person in Europe and £2 million worldwide.
- Helicopter search and rescue: searching a wide area is usually far more expensive than simply rescuing a casualty from a known location.

It is also worth bearing in mind that whilst on holiday you might decide to sign up for an activity that you had not planned to undertake. For instance, a day or two of white-water rafting is a popular activity with some trekkers at the end of their holiday. Does your trekking policy include watersports? You might find it difficult to extend an existing policy whilst you are abroad.

If you are planning to undertake several trips every year, an annual policy might prove more cost-effective than several short policies. Also, if any spontaneous opportunities come your way, you will be able to take off at a moment's notice.

Although the insurance company sells you the policy, it is unlikely to handle any emergencies directly. This part of the insurance cover is contracted out to an assistance company. The assistance company is available for general medical advice, rescue, repatriation and situations like lost passports. A competent assistance company can be a useful ally. However, if they do not have expertise in the part of the world that you are in, the organisation might sub-contract a second company to look after you. In the event that you request aid, this contracting-out procedure inevitably lengthens the chain of command. It may cause delays as faxes fly between the three companies until the financial cost of assisting you is finally nailed down. Don't forget that you may be separated from the insurance and assistance companies by up to 12 time zones. Delays like these can endanger life in an emergency: a comprehensive policy bought from an experienced and reputable company is almost always worth paying for. Uniquely, British Mountaineering Council officers sometimes become directly involved with co-ordinating search and rescue operations when holders of this organisation's policies are reported as missing.

‘ An airplane is a flying Petri dish, full of germs: be well-rested before you climb aboard. Kathmandu will bombard you with germs; if you are rested and healthy you will adapt quickly to most of them. ’

Mark Twight

Find out your assistance company's telephone number and the relevant international dialling code. The telephone number is usually included on the policy form. It might be a wise idea to distribute the details of your policy to at least two other individuals in your group. If you are travelling on your own, think about attaching this information to a waterproofed swing tag on the outside of your rucksack. However, the advantages of this ploy will need to be balanced against someone reading the information and using it for their own devices.

Immunisations

Vaccines are highly effective in preventing disease. Some vaccinations require a three-month course of injections, so try to plan ahead. Up-to-date information is best obtained from your GP or a professional organisation that is familiar with the risks of disease and the effectiveness of the appropriate vaccination. The following information is a general guide to recommended vaccinations for adults. *Appendix A includes addresses of professional medical organisations.*

GUIDE TO RECOMMENDED IMMUNISATIONS

Essential:
Tetanus, Polio, Typhoid.

Highly recommended:
Hepatitis A.

Consider:
Diphtheria, Hepatitis B, Japanese Encephalitis, Meningitis A + C, Rabies pre-exposure, Yellow Fever and other vaccinations.

The injections that you decide to have will depend on many things including:

- The country you are visiting
- Your health
- Existing vaccination status
- The duration of expected contact with local people
- The activity you are planning to engage in
- The standard of accommodation you anticipate using

Note: some countries insist on vaccination certificates, so check with the relevant embassy to see if any such regulations are in place. *Appendix A includes UK embassy details for countries which are popular with mountain travellers.*

Visiting Your Doctor And Dentist

If you have a pre-existing medical condition or are planning to undertake a trek or climb for the first time (or the first time in a while) then it is sensible to visit your family doctor (GP) for advice and a check-up. Your visit will be even more productive if your GP has personal experience of the type of activity you are planning to undertake. There is also no harm in paying a visit to your dentist: whilst a competent doctor can be hard to find in certain developing countries, tracking down a competent dentist can sometimes prove impossible. Some travellers also make a point of visiting their GP on their return for a general check-up. If you are leaving children behind it is worth depositing a signed emergency treatment consent form with the GP and also the temporary guardian, although the latter might necessitate the involvement of a solicitor.

Personal Medication

It is essential to obtain and carry an adequate supply of all medications you regularly take, including an additional amount to cover unexpected delays. Remember to carry copies of any prescription orders. If you have a specific medical condition (such as diabetes) or an allergy to a certain medication or insect bite, it's advisable to inform someone else in your group. You might also want to wear an identity bracelet and carry an information card in your passport. Always read the instructions supplied with medicines. It's worth dividing all your medicines in half so that equal amounts can be carried in your hand and aircraft hold luggage. The same tactic can be applied whilst on the trek or climb.

Although a doctor's letter – stating the need for these medicines and other medical equipment such as syringes – is a useful piece of documentation to have, it may be rendered null and void if the medicines you are carrying are on the list of controlled drugs for the country you are visiting. You might want to obtain a copy of this list from the relevant embassy before you visit your GP.

Travellers who wear glasses are encouraged to pack a spare pair (preferably in a hard case) as well as a copy of their lens prescription. Trekkers who wear contact lenses usually carry a quantity of cleaning solution sufficient to last the entire trip.

COLD WEATHER INJURIES

With the correct clothing and equipment, and an adequate daily intake of calories and water, the majority of cold weather injuries can be avoided. It is

> In many parts of the world the only form of safe sex is on your own with a condom on.
>
> *Dr David Hillebrandt*

> *It's not unusual to have to order meals twice in a lodge, in which case you'll either get two of whatever you ordered (no bad thing) or the kitchen staff will rush your order and it won't get the thorough cooking that it requires. Be warned: if you eat under-cooked food, you'll probably end up quick-stepping to the nearest toilet with a dose of food poisoning.*

Seb Mankelow

worth bearing in mind that every action causes a reaction: for example, leaving sunglasses off on a glacier (even in cloudy weather) is a sure-fire way to encourage the onset of snow blindness.

Hypothermia

Hypothermia is present in a person when their core temperature drops to below 35°C. The normal temperature of the core is approximately 37°C so you can see that it does not require much of a reduction in core temperature to induce this condition. To prevent hypothermia, ensure that:

- Your outer clothing protects you from wet and wind
- You are wearing a sufficient number of dry inner layers to keep warm
- You maintain a regular intake of food and drink

However, in the mountains, these seemingly straightforward precautions can sometimes be difficult to implement. Hypothermia can creep up on an individual with very little warning, and it is almost impossible to self-diagnose the condition especially if you have never suffered from it before. Young people and the elderly are particularly vulnerable.

Hypothermia usually announces itself by causing:

- A loss of judgement
- A slurring of speech
- A general denial on the part of the victim that there is anything wrong

The person suffering from the early stages of hypothermia may shiver, which is the body's way of generating more heat. As the individual deteriorates, shivering ceases.

The more quickly hypothermia is identified, the sooner treatment can begin, and the more rapidly recovery will take place. A person with mild hypothermia (which occurs when the body's core temperature is between 35°C and 32°C) will often be able to make a full recovery in the field. Seek shelter or erect a tent. Encourage the victim to drink plenty of hot, sweet liquid. Indeed, it is strongly advisable for all members of the group to take shelter and to drink at this time, in order to prevent additional cases of hypothermia developing. A lightweight bothy bag or 'zdarski' refuge that is capable of accommodating every member of the team can prove invaluable in situations where tents are not being carried by the group. *You can read more about zdarski refuges and managing enforced bivouacs in Chapter 3.*

It is best to assume that the victim's clothes are damp. If a sufficient amount of spare clothing exists in the group, then all the patient's clothes should be changed (whilst preserving his modesty). If only one dry layer can be found, put it on next to the skin. A hat and a pair of mitts (pre-warmed by someone else) can often work wonders at this stage. So does morale-boosting conversation which encourages the victim to talk. Do whatever is necessary to prevent the victim from lapsing into unconsciousness. In more advanced cases of hypothermia, zip two sleeping bags together and place the victim inside, along with another (healthy) person. Recovery may take several hours. Do not rub or massage the victim, or place him near a fire, as these actions will only serve to worsen his condition: massaging sends cold blood to the already chilled core, whilst artificial sources of heat encourage the core to open up skin blood vessels. By doing this the body will lose any residual warmth.

Severe hypothermia (below 32°C) in a remote setting, far from a medical centre, is a very serious situation. If the patient is unconscious, he should be placed in the recovery position if possible. Bear in mind that the body is able to slow itself down to such an extent that a pulse may be barely discernible. An unconscious person with severe hypothermia and no detectable pulse must always be assumed to be alive until a medical doctor with appropriate experience has said otherwise. A victim of hypothermia is not dead until he is warm and dead. Warming a person with severe hypothermia is fraught with problems, and should be done in a hospital. *Appendix E contains a list of books that give detailed information on dealing with severe hypothermia.*

Frostbite

As with hypothermia, frostbite – which is literally the freezing of a body part – is often preventable. Wearing adequate clothing that protects against sub-zero temperatures and icy winds is essential. In low temperatures, the extremities (hands, feet and face) are most at risk. A balaclava or face mask will protect the nose and cheeks. Ensure that mittens and boots are dry and that they contain sufficient insulation to ward off the temperatures you expect to encounter. A second set of gloves (or even socks) can act as spares in the event that your mitts become lost or soaked. It is vital to maintain an adequate level of hydration, particularly at altitude.

Even with such precautions, mild frostbite (commonly known as 'frostnip') can occur without warning. One give-away sign is the waxy, white patch that develops over the affected spot. Keeping a close eye on your colleagues will help to ensure that frostnip is detected early on. Immediate

> Apply sunblock as soon as the sun hits you when you are travelling on snow. Remember to apply it to easy-to-forget places like the nostrils.

Dr John Mitchell

re-warming, by placing a bare hand against the affected area, is the recommended treatment. As soon as the skin begins to flush, the area must be covered and insulated so that it cannot re-freeze.

The same cannot be said of so-called 'superficial' frostbite, where the flesh becomes frozen below the surface of the skin. There is nothing superficial about this complaint, which is very serious indeed. It is most common in the hands and feet. These areas often remain covered during the day. This prevents them from being inspected regularly. The victim of superficial frostbite may choose to ignore any loss of sensation in these areas, as he may not want to delay the rest of the party by removing the mitt or boot for a visual examination. Such reticence can be costly, as in a few hours frostnip can turn into irreversible frostbite.

If frostbite is discovered, a decision about whether to treat the affected part immediately or at a later stage will have to be made. Frostbite often occurs on mountaineering expeditions, many days away from a place where the victim can be evacuated by helicopter or stretcher. In these instances it may be better to leave the affected area frozen (especially if it is a foot) whilst taking every precaution to ensure that the injury does not spread to unaffected tissue. The reason for this is simple: as soon as re-warming takes place, the damaged part will usually be far too painful for the victim to use.

If you allow your hands to get cold, it can be difficult to re-warm them

Re-warming may commence when the victim is in a sheltered environment from where there is no need to use the affected part again. Clearly, if a guaranteed evacuation to a medical centre is only a short time away, a decision will need to be made as to whether to re-warm the frostbitten appendage in the mountain environment or wait until the victim is in the care of experienced doctors.

There are plenty of old wives' tales about curing frostbite. These include: rubbing the affected part with snow; placing the limb in freezing water; and holding the damaged area over a fire. All these are complete rubbish, and will only serve to make the condition even more serious. It is usually recommended to encourage rapid warming by placing the limb in hand-hot (39-42˚C) water for periods of 20 minutes until it becomes soft. Take care not to scald the patient. If hot water is not available, the affected part may be warmed in a sleeping bag, or against the abdomen, groin, or armpits for several hours. Above 5500m, oxygen should be given if it is available. Thawing may be extremely painful. Painkillers can be taken.

After re-warming has taken place, the affected area must be protected against further re-freezing. Ideally it should be lightly bandaged. It is vital to keep the skin as clean as possible in order to minimise the risk of infection. Should infection occur, antibiotics will be required. The victim should be encouraged to move the damaged limb but not undertake any tasks with it. After thawing, the tissue will swell and giant blisters may form. These should be allowed to settle, in order to reveal discoloured or black tissue. After several weeks this shell will separate. If the frostbite is superficial, new skin will appear. If deep frostbite has occurred, the blackened appendage will gradually separate: an unsightly but painless process. Surgery may be delayed for weeks or even months.

Sun And Snow Blindness

Wearing a pair of sunglasses or goggles that filter out 100% of ultra-violet (UV) radiation is the best possible insurance against this debilitating complaint. Snow blindness sometimes feels akin to having sandpaper rubbed into the eyeball. It can be agonising. Painkillers may be taken until recovery occurs. Every effort should be made to prevent light from entering the damaged eye(s): a thick piece of dark cloth cut into the shape of an eye mask (like the ones given out by some airlines as an aid to sleep) normally does the trick. Prevention is better than cure: a spare pair of glasses or goggles can prove to be a very useful piece of kit on both treks and climbs. If the victim has to be moved – and needs to see in order to do so – then dark sunglasses should be worn in order to minimise the amount of light

> I take a matted tarp-style space blanket along as a piece of safety gear. It lasts much longer than tissue-weight foil varieties. The blanket can be used as a short-term shelter for two or three people in heavy rain or snow. It can also cover gear at camps.

Sue Fear

able to strike at the already damaged eye. Eye drops containing a local anaesthetic may also be administered. Emergency sunglasses can be made from a piece of foam or card with narrow slits to allow vision. *You can read more about different types of eye protection in Chapter 13.*

HOT WEATHER ILLNESSES

When we think about medical care in the mountain environment, it is easy to dismiss as negligible the chance of contracting a hot weather illness. However, a quick flick through an atlas will confirm that certain mountains (including the equatorial giants of East Africa, the Atlas mountains in Morocco and rock climbing areas such as Wadi Rum) require the climber or trekker to experience hot weather. The human body requires up to three weeks of inactivity to adjust to a sweltering environment, so mountain travellers who visit this type of destination for just a fortnight already face an uphill battle.

It is also possible to succumb to a hot weather illness in a distinctly non-tropical environment. The approaches to many of the world's highest mountains require the trekker to experience temperatures well in excess of those encountered whilst sunbathing on a Mediterranean beach. Furthermore, the reflected heat generated on glaciers and snow slopes can stop even the most determined mountaineer in his tracks.

An emergency pair of sunglasses: prevention is better than cure

Dehydration And Heat Exhaustion

The colour of your urine is your most reliable guide as to whether you are drinking an adequate amount of water. If your urine is pale in colour, then you are probably drinking the required amount. Temperature, humidity, and level of acclimatisation (to the climate and altitude) all play a part in determining how much water your body needs. In certain situations, six litres or more every day might be required.

In tropical conditions, salt deficiency can be a major problem: adding a pinch of salt (approximately half of a level teaspoon for every litre of water) to all of your drinks will help counter-balance the salt that is lost though excessive sweating. This amount of salt is unlikely to taint the contents of your water bottle.

Dehydration and an inadequate intake of salt can lead to heat exhaustion, a condition that initially feels similar to the state one wakes up in after a heavy night of drinking. Heat exhaustion can advance to include headache, dizziness, nausea and vomiting. Importantly, mental function is *not* impaired in a patient with heat exhaustion. The victim's temperature does not increase very much (if at all) and certainly does not exceed 40°C as the term implies, the patient is literally exhausted from the heat

Place the victim of heat exhaustion in a cool environment by rigging a temporary shade with poles and a tent flysheet, or by erecting a tent (load sleeping bags onto the roof to reduce the internal temperature). Supply the patient with plenty of lightly salted fluids. These actions should bring about a rapid recovery. If not, or if the victim passes out more than momentarily, then assume the patient is suffering from the more severe heat illness known as heatstroke.

Heatstroke

Also known as sunstroke, heatstroke is a potentially life-threatening illness for which prompt treatment is vital if the victim is to make a full recovery. It might help to understand a little about body mechanics in order to realise why heatstroke is so serious. The victim of heatstroke loses his ability to cool down. This is life-threatening because normally the body produces a vast amount of heat. It has been estimated that an 'average' person with an 'average' metabolic rate who stored all the heat he generated in a 24 hour period might see his core temperature rise from 37°C to around 88°C. Initial signs of heatstroke include confusion, a lack of co-ordination and irrational behaviour. These are followed by drowsiness and unconsciousness. Without prompt treatment, death can occur.

Unlike patients with heat exhaustion, victims of heatstroke suffer a rapid rise in body temperature beyond 41°C. Heatstroke victims might be covered in sweat, or have a dry skin. The pulse will be rapid. Treatment for a victim with heatstroke in a mountain environment is often much easier to administer than if it occurs in the classic desert setting. The victim should be placed in the shade. If the victim is unconscious, place him in the recovery position. Clothing should be removed, and cool, wet materials (such as wet clothing or a sleeping bag liner that has been soaked in cool water) should be laid over the patient. The naked victim can also be sprayed with cool water. The most effective treatment is to wet the head. If you find yourself on a glacier with no running water, then placing snow and ice on a dark surface (such as a tent flysheet) will quickly produce meltwater if the sun is shining. Do not give painkillers or apply ice. (Ice can actually raise the core temperature, and delay the cooling process.) During this initial cooling phase, massaging the feet and hands will encourage the now-cooled blood within them to return more quickly to the internal organs and brain. Once the body's temperature has dropped below 39°C, a balance between further cooling and avoiding hypothermia needs to be struck. A victim of heatstroke is still a patient even when he has regained consciousness. He should be evacuated to hospital as soon as possible, as the internal organs may have failed or been damaged as a result of the heat.

Protection From The Sun

The burning effect of the sun in the mountain environment, especially at altitude, is far more potent than on any beach. According to one cancer research centre, ultraviolet (UV) light is 50% more intense at 3000m than at sea level. Protection is the number one priority, and constant vigilance is necessary. It is strongly recommend that a sunblock or very high strength sunscreen is applied to all exposed skin. The nose, ears and lips are particularly susceptible. The nose can be protected by a piece of leather clipped to the sunglasses, whilst sunblock needs to be re-applied on a regular basis to the ears and lips. Snow reflects UV back onto the face and can cause severe sunburn, so take special care when travelling on snow. Most sun products have sun protection factor (SPF) ratings. It is important to understand what the SPF rating means. A cream with an SPF rating of 10 (commonly described as 'Factor 10') allows you to stay out in the sun for 10 times longer (without burning) than had you no cream on at all. So if you normally start to burn in the sun after 15 minutes, an application of Factor 10 cream would enable you to stay in the sun for 150 minutes before beginning to burn. It is important to note that applying additional Factor 10 after 150 minutes would make no difference at all: your body will have gained all it can from that level of protection, and is now ready to burn. The only effective protection at that stage would be to get out of the sun, either by putting on some clothes, or by heading for a piece of shade. For this reason, people visiting mountain regions are advised to apply a cream that has an SPF of 25 or more: developing a 'safe' tan in the high mountains is a very hit-and-miss affair, even for the most experienced sun-worshipper. Re-applying the cream during the time when it is still effective will ensure that the benefits of the treatment do not wear off prematurely. If you have an old bottle of suncream in your bathroom cabinet take a moment to check its production date. The shelf life of these types of sun products is usually only two to three years.

SPF ratings only gauge the level of protection against UV-B rays. Whilst UV-B causes sunburn, UV-A is responsible for ageing and skin cancer, so it is definitely worth spending extra money on a product that has a high level of protection for both. Protection against UV-A rays is usually shown using a star system. In addition, some outdoor clothing manufacturers are now adding SPF or Universal Protection Factor (UPF) ratings to their clothing. *You can read more about dressing to protect against the sun in Chapter 13.*

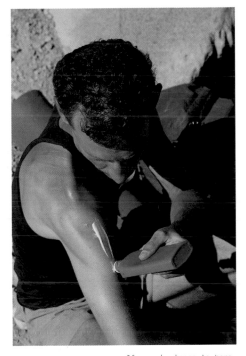

If you do choose to bare skin, use plenty of very high strength sunscreen

The sun is at its most intense between 10am and 3pm, so do everything you can to minimise your exposure to the sun during these hours. On your trip it may prove possible to rise before dawn, set out at first light, and enjoy a long lunch in the shade of a rock or tree between midday and 2pm.

A person suffering from sunburn is strongly advised to drink plenty of liquids, and to keep the affected area out of the sun. Calamine lotion may be applied and painkillers can be taken.

OTHER INJURIES AND ILLNESSES
Diarrhoea
Adopting a fastidious attitude towards what you eat and drink will minimise your chance of becoming sick on a trip. Nevertheless, a bout of 'Kathmandu

Quickstep', 'Delhi Belly' or 'Montezuma's Revenge' can sometimes be a near-certainty on a journey where alien foods and drinks are being consumed. The good news is that most encounters with so-called 'Traveller's Diarrhoea' are short-lived. In these situations, most sufferers can initially do little more than sip plenty of purified water (to offset the fluid being lost with each motion) and rest. This is easier said than done if you are travelling along a bumpy road, or trekking to the next night's camp. If you are experiencing a bowel movement more frequently than you can tolerate, or are in a place (such as an aircraft) where frequent visits to the toilet are not an option, then consider taking anti-diarrhoeal medication such as Loperamide (Immodium) as per the manufacturer's instructions.

In an ideal world, an individual suffering from diarrhoea for more than 48 hours would seek the opinion of a doctor. However, in many mountain situations this simply is not practical. The usual recourse is to take the appropriate antibiotic from your medical kit. All GPs have up-to-date treatment guidelines for traveller's diarrhoea. *Chapter 9 has advice on which foods to avoid in order to minimise the chance of contracting traveller's diarrhoea, whilst Appendix D includes a list of suggested drugs to treat the condition.*

Haemorrhoids

Rectal bleeding, which is often spotted on toilet paper, may be caused by an exacerbation of haemorrhoids. This can be brought on by an increase in altitude and normally responds to regular anti-haemorrhoidal treatment. Anyone over the age of 45 who experiences rectal bleeding is advised to seek medical advice, as is anyone under the age of 45 who has a family history of bowel cancer. Blood or slime that is mixed in with the faeces can indicate an infection of the bowel. If this occurs, seek medical advice as soon as possible. Perianal dermititis (a sore bottom) can be avoided by cleaning oneself with plain water or a medicated wet tissue after using toilet paper. Note that it has been known for individuals to become allergic to certain medicated tissues during the course of their trip, which has then led to the onset of the very condition they had been striving to avoid.

Bites And Stings

Bites and stings from insects are often part and parcel of treks and climbs that take place below 3000m. Some insects, such as the Aedes mosquito that transmits Dengue fever, bite during the day. Others, including the female Anopheline mosquito that transmits malaria, only bite from dusk to dawn. If you are travelling or trekking in an area and suspect the presence of biting

> I use vinegar (carried in a dropper bottle) to remove leeches.

Jerry Gore

insects, cover up all exposed skin, especially around the ankles. Apply an insect repellent to the cuffs of your long-sleeved shirt, the hem of your trousers, and all over your neckerchief. Note that some insects can bite through thin fabrics. In certain places you might need to wear a net over your face, but a hat sprayed with insect repellent usually proves enough of a deterrent in most mountain environments. Insect repellent can be applied to the hands and face. Avoid applying repellent to your forehead because when you sweat you will 'wash' the repellent into your eyes. At night, sleep under a net that has been treated with an insecticide such as Pemethrin. If you visit the toilet in the small hours, remember to cover up again. Apply repellent to your exposed nether regions – mosquitoes love toilets. Ownership of a pee bottle may remove the need to leave the sanctity of your net during the night.

If you are planning to travel in or through a malarial region (even if only for a few days) then it is important to get hold of the most recent information on the correct prophylactic medicine to take. Seek advice from an appropriately trained professional. When you have obtained the appropriate course of medicine, start taking the tablets as directed. Some prophylactic treatments need to be started as much as two weeks before arrival. Take the tablets whilst you are in the malarial zone, and continue with the course for the recommended length of time after leaving the region. It might seem strange to have to continue with the course after your trip. However, if you have been bitten, malarial parasites can incubate in the liver for many weeks before entering the bloodstream to cause symptoms of malaria. Travel to malarial areas should be avoided during pregnancy.

If you are bitten by an animal, clean and dress the wound. A course of appropriate antibiotic is highly recommended to prevent infection. Consider the possibility that the animal could have rabies. Unless you can be certain that the animal is not rabid, seek professional medical help urgently.

Burns

A burn resulting from a fire or stove is a thankfully uncommon occurrence in the mountain environment. However, given that most mountain travellers walk around in layer-upon-layer of synthetic clothing, the consequences of any contact with a naked flame could be catastrophic. In bad weather, many mountaineers are forced to cook inside their nylon tents, which increases the risk. If an article of your clothing does catch fire, then immediately drop to the ground and roll over in order to smother the flames. Bear in mind that it is not possible to gauge the severity of a burn until 48 hours after the accident, and that pain is not a reliable indication of the severity of a burn.

If you suffer a minor burn to your skin, then immerse the affected area in cold water for at least one hour. Replace the water periodically as it warms up. 60 minutes might seem a ridiculously long time, but the water will take the heat out of the burn. An hour spent bathing and cooling at the time of the accident is likely to spare you several days of suffering. The main problem with burns is infection. After bathing, clean the site with Betadine-soaked gauze. Apply a Bactigras dressing (other types of dressing stick to burned skin). Make every effort to have the burn checked after 48 hours by a competent medical professional.

An evacuation to a hospital must be organised immediately for someone who suffers a large burn. Wrap the area in 'cling film' or cover in a piece of clean plastic and hold in position with a loose bandage. Give the victim plenty of fluids, but do not immerse the affected part(s) in water. If you suffer a burn to the hands, face or genitals seek specialist advice. A thin smear of petroleum jelly (Vaseline) is the ideal dressing for a facial burn.

Trauma

The treatment of trauma and of specific fractures is beyond the scope of this book, and the interested reader is strongly advised to attend an appropriate mountain first aid course. Broken bones need to be immobilised in order to reduce pain and bleeding. If a member is incapacitated – as a result of trauma in a remote environment days or weeks from outside support – then difficult decisions may need to be made. It is always important not to endanger the lives of other members of the party. *Books such as the BMC's 'Safety on Mountains' contain further information on this subject and can be found listed in Appendix E.*

Notes For This Chapter

1. Self diagnosis is to be heavily discouraged, even when the patient is a qualified doctor. This applies to every medical condition. Precise clinical diagnosis without modern laboratory facilities can be very difficult, even for highly skilled medical doctors. Many different diseases can mimic each other with their symptoms.

2. Anyone taking any medication should be aware of potential recorded side-effects, written details of which should be supplied with the drug by the dispensing chemist.

Fevers And Pain

A non-mercury digital or forehead thermometer is a useful piece of equipment to carry, as a patient with a temperature greater than 38.5°C has a significant fever. Depending on other signs and symptoms present, professional medical attention may need to be sought. Pain relief tablets may be taken for fevers, headaches and general aches, as well as muscle and joint strains and sprains. However, powerful painkillers can sometimes mask the symptoms of altitude illness. *You can read about altitude illness in Chapter 10.*

Wounds

Open wounds of any type take a long time to heal, particularly at altitude. People with even a moderate wound at altitude should consider descending in order to promote healing. Wounds must be kept clean at all times, and this can also be difficult to achieve in the mountain environment. An antibiotic may need to be taken if the wound becomes infected. A worsening of the pain, redness, swelling and a wound that feels hot to the touch all indicate possible infection. Be aware that hand injuries can cause damage to tendons, nerves or blood vessels. Wounds to the hand, and large wounds, should be seen by a doctor as soon as possible.

YOUR QUESTIONS ANSWERED

I'm on a trek and my boots are hurting my feet. What can I do?

Rubbing on the heel: check that the boot has a plastic heel cup by squeezing the heel. If you meet resistance then it probably does and you may proceed with this treatment. Place the heel of the boot in a plastic bag and dip it into a pan of boiling water for several minutes. Take care not to scald your hand. Remove the boot from the water and the bag, put your foot in the boot, lace it up and stand facing uphill on a slope. Ask a friend to mould the softened heel to the shape of your foot with his hand and hold in position until the boot material cools and hardens.. With the heel of the boot now customised to your foot, there should be less chance of rubbing.

Feet slipping forward in boots, causing pain to toes: this means that the boot is too large. Add a second insole to the boot (by cutting a pair out of a foam mat) and/or wear an extra sock. Alternatively, an elasticated 'Tubigrip' style support may be doubled up from just above the ankle bone to under the arch of the foot. Fattening the ankle in this way might. allow the boot to hold the heel in place, preventing slippage.

Reddened 'hot spot' forming: apply a piece of sticking plaster to the skin. A second piece of smooth, shiny tape can be applied over this. The sticking plaster gives the shiny tape something to adhere to; the shiny tape allows the boots to slide over the area, which prevents further rubbing.

Blister formed: only remove the liquid in the blister if absolutely necessary. This can be done by inserting a sterile needle and drawing the liquid up into a syringe. If you do not have a syringe then sterilise a sewing needle over a flame, prick the blister and squeeze the liquid out of the hole. Take care not to touch the area. A proprietary cushioning and rehydrating product (e.g. 'Second Skin') may then be applied to the wound. Cover with a sticking plaster, keep clean and re-dress daily. If the blister bursts, protect the new, exposed skin with a product such as 'Second Skin' and cover with a plaster.

> Take your time in difficult situations.
> For instance, if you are not sure of
> your route, take your time over
> map-reading; cast about in a logical,
> measured way.

Tim Salmon

Situations To Avoid

Awareness of, and experience in dealing with, potential hazards is built up over a lifetime of repeated exposure to the mountain environment. There is no 'quick fix' for this, which is why experienced leaders and guides are worth their weight in gold when it comes to negotiating a potentially hazardous situation. So what can inexperienced people – particularly those travelling independently – do in order to tip the odds in their favour? Precautions that can be taken against some of the more common hazards are described here.

MOUNTAIN HAZARDS

Weather

In poor weather, you will need to decide for yourself whether to delay crossing a pass, or postpone a summit attempt. The fact that the people around you may continue on is no guarantee that things will turn out for the best, as the infamous events on the Nepalese side of Everest on May 10th 1996 – when five climbers died – stand testament to. Do what you can to find out what the typical weather pattern is for the area that you find

> Know the
> likely
> climatic
> conditions.
> For example,
> is it the
> monsoon
> season? What
> stage is the
> monsoon at? Is
> it continual
> torrential
> rain, morning
> rain, or
> afternoon
> rain?

Henry Todd

9:30 A.M. WEATHER FORECAST
FOR 05 /12/ 92

PREDICTED WORST
STORM IN 10 YEARS...

- WINDS UP TO 110 MPH (160 KM)
- HEAVY SNOWFALL ON WEST SLOPES
- WARMER TEMPERATURES
- DURATION: 48   HOURS

WELCOME TO DENALI !!

Weather forecasting
is rarely this
accurate - or
available

yourself in. One of the most reliable sources of such information can be the people who live in the region. For example, it is quite usual for clouds to roll into Himalayan valleys during the mid-afternoon of the pre-monsoon and post-monsoon seasons. If you know that this type of weather is normal, you will feel more confident about pushing on at 4pm. By contrast, the formation of a lenticular (crescent-shaped) cloud over the summit of Mont Blanc is a virtual guarantee of bad weather in the ensuing hours and days.

Unseasonal Snowfall

Snow can fall in the mountains at any time of year, making travel difficult or impossible for ill-equipped parties. Unseasonal snowfall can also slow groups down in unexpected ways. For example, if pack animals are unable to graze overnight because of snow or frozen ground, their handlers may be reluctant to drive them on the following day. A little flexibility in your schedule will absorb such eventualities. If you plan to trek at altitude, ensure that your clothing and equipment is able to withstand unexpected snowfall. If all members of the party – including porters – have the correct gear then this will reduce the chance of anyone becoming cold, wet and uncomfortable. *Porter issues are discussed in Chapter 4. Equipment is described in Chapter 13.*

‘Never underestimate the great distance some avalanches can travel, especially when choosing a place to set up camp.’

Tim Macartney-Snape

Glaciers

For people on mountaineering expeditions, a working knowledge of glaciers – and how to negotiate them – is essential in order to allow the party to proceed safely. Skills such as crevasse rescue are usually learnt on your first visit to a glaciated region. Traditionally, many climbers and walkers learnt the rudiments of glacier travel in places like the European and Southern Alps, before moving onto bigger things in the Andes, Pamirs and Himalaya. Today, it is not uncommon for someone's first big mountain experience outside of their own country to be on something like one of the so-called 'Trekking Peaks' in Nepal (most of which are anything but suitable for trekkers). If you decide to head for a high altitude or glaciated region with a commercial operator, but you do not have any previous experience of glacier travel, then at the very least make sure that the company you sign up with is aware of your skill level at the time of booking. That way you will be able to receive the necessary instruction from your guide before setting out for the summit. However, learning new skills at high altitude is not ideal and reputable operators insist on prior experience. This can be gained by attending an alpine preparation course. Incidentally, this type of programme works equally well for independent teams as well as people planning to join an organised trip.

Avalanche

Avalanches can occur in any mountain region where there is a build-up of snow on a slope. It is a fallacy to believe that avalanches only occur on steep-sided mountains, and are therefore of no concern to the trekker. Avalanches are most likely to occur on slopes that are at an angle of 20° to 50°; exactly the type of slope that trekkers regularly find themselves on. Nor do avalanches occur only in environments that are the sole preserve of the mountaineer: in 1995, 25 trekkers, staff and local people died as a result of an avalanche in the popular trekking valley of Gokyo, close to Mount Everest. It is wise to treat any slope loaded with even a small amount of new snow as potentially avalanche prone: a tiny avalanche might be sufficient to sweep you off your feet. Some places are notorious for their avalanche danger: the section of trail between Deorali and Bhaga, on the trail into Nepal's Annapurna Sanctuary, is noted for the avalanches that slide off the neighbouring peak of Hiunchuli.

It is normal practice for mountaineers to be familiar with avalanche evaluation techniques, and they may be equipped with avalanche transceivers and probes. However, the trekker is unlikely to have such knowledge or equipment. Most avalanches result from heavy snowfall or deposits of windblown snow that have accumulated over a sustained period of time. In these situations, the greatest threat of avalanche normally continues for up to 48 hours after the snowfall has ended. Trekking routes may be threatened by avalanches that begin far above the track; these slides are unlikely to be triggered by the victim or another individual but rather initiated spontaneously by the sheer weight of snow. The upshot of all this is that it is difficult for someone without detailed knowledge of the area to assess fully the avalanche risk. Soliciting an opinion from someone who knows the region intimately can be useful after heavy snowfall in order to identify potentially dangerous places. Such a person could be a guide who is passing through with a group, or a person who lives in the nearest village. If in any doubt, avoid the area.

'First time climbers in the Himalaya need to be aware of potential snow problems. There is often a great risk of avalanche which can be difficult to see from low down on the mountain. It is vital that each section of the route is assessed.'

Smiler Cuthbertson

Hidden crevasses can present problems; there are actually seven people in this photograph

Some river crossings are too dangerous to ford

River Crossings

A river can be a frightening and hazardous obstacle. As well as making all members of the party cold and wet, the river's current may be strong enough to sweep an individual off his feet. If you find yourself needing to cross a river, study your map and seek advice as to whether there is a bridge in the vicinity. A 10km walk to a crossing point is preferable to a soaking or worse.

If a river crossing is inevitable, then consider all your options. Is there a village nearby? If so, you might be able to rent a horse and rider to take your party across. If not, check the time of day. Mountain rivers are at their lowest level at dawn: perhaps waiting until early morning would make the river safer to cross? Investigate the river in both directions to find the safest crossing point. Riverbends are often deep and powerful on their outside edge. Narrow gorges concentrate the full force of the water into one spot. However, some gorges may be so narrow that it is actually possible to jump from one bank to the other. If you decide to do this, take your rucksack off and arrange for the last person to hurl the sacks over. If the sacks are too heavy to throw, pass the equipment across piece-by-piece.

If you have no option but to wade, then the safest place is often at the river's widest point. This is because the power of the river will be spread over the largest area. Try and pick a spot that has shallow banks on both sides. This will make getting into and out of the river easier. A 'third leg', in the form of a trekking pole or stout stick, can be an invaluable aid when crossing a river.

HOW TO CROSS A RIVER WITHOUT A ROPE

Whilst it is always worth walking a considerable distance to find a bridge or other safe method of crossing a river, sometimes you may have no choice but to wade across. There are various methods of crossing a river without using a rope; the 'Line Abreast' technique is described here.

Before you set foot in the river, try to gauge its depth. Provided that you do not expect the water to come above the waist (and if it does then you might want to re-think your plans) remove all the clothing on your lower half, and put on a pair of waterproof trousers. Take off your socks and remove boot insoles but put your boots back on; the last thing you want to do is to cut your foot on the river bed. If you have gaiters, wear them. Secure the contents of your rucksack but leave the hipbelt undone so that the sack can be slipped off your shoulders and used as a buoyancy aid if you are swept away.

Everyone then needs to line up on the shore, facing the opposite bank. The strongest person should be at the upstream end of the line in order to deflect the current. Link arms, and reinforce this by passing a branch or trekking pole through the linked arms. On entering the water, the party should aim to shuffle forward at the speed of the slowest person. As you approach the opposite bank, avoid the temptation to break rank and dive for the shoreline. Exit the river one at a time in an orderly fashion. Strip off your wet clothes, empty your boots and dress quickly. Keep alert for signs of hypothermia. *You can read more about hypothermia in Chapter 5.*

Rockfall

Rockfall is a far more common threat to backpackers than avalanche. On encountering an area that shows signs of previous rockfall, it is wise to cross the danger zone one at a time. In some situations it may be better to wait to cross at first light the next day: rocks often fall in the afternoon when the ice and snow holding them in place melts as a result of the action of the sun. At dawn, the rocks are more likely to be frozen to the mountain.

If you are caught in a rockfall, you will need to make an instant decision as to whether to look up and dodge the flying rocks, run and take cover behind a boulder or sit down and put your rucksack above your head. It is worth bearing in mind that many mountain roads are cut into unstable hillsides and so vehicles and their occupants are also at risk.

Helmets are not the sole preserve of mountaineers: scramblers - and on occasion backpackers - also need to consider using them

Benightment

Benightment (being caught out in the dark) usually occurs as a result of an overly ambitious plan or unexpected incident. If the route ahead is certain then it might be possible to continue your journey, especially if you have a torch. However, if you are in any doubt about the direction to take or if you have been injured, then you may have no choice but to sit out the night. *You can read about enforced bivouacs in Chapter 3.*

Other Mountain Users

Trekkers and mountaineers can themselves present a hazard, both directly and indirectly. Someone above you may drop an item of equipment, or dislodge a stone. If you find yourself climbing or scrambling on a route that is congested with other climbers, hold back, give others space, and consider sheltering under an overhang. Better still, wear a helmet.

Mountain users might get themselves into difficulty, suffer an injury or become ill. In these instances, the unwritten code of assisting someone in trouble is always adhered to by all responsible people. A loud shout, or repeated blasts on a whistle, are two quick ways to summon attention.

OTHER HAZARDS

There are a number of additional hazards that the trekker or climber might encounter. Most of these are thankfully rare.

Animals

Domestic animals, especially dogs, can be a frightening hazard. Guard dogs are used by many people living in remote areas and of course there is no way for the lay person to tell whether the animal is carrying rabies. Dogs can be quite terrifying so keep a stick or trekking pole to hand as your priority is to avoid being bitten. The best tactic is avoidance: steer clear of private property. If approached by a dog, pick up a stone and raise your hand as if to throw it. In the majority of cases the dog will then keep its distance, providing you keep yours. If you are forced to walk past a property that is guarded by a threatening dog, call out in order to alert the owner to your presence.

In certain parts of the world, animals will scavenge for food around campsites. You can minimise this hazard by not scattering or burying waste food, and by sealing your provisions in boxes and bags. Even this is no guarantee that they will not be broken into: food boxes must be buried in snow and ice on Denali, to prevent ravens from gorging on precious supplies.

Trekkers and climbers heading into bear country are strongly advised to seek the advice of local rangers on appropriate walking and camping procedures. On mountains (such as Mt Kenya) where there is a risk of running into wild animals such as elephant and buffalo, it makes sense to hire a knowledgeable local guide.

Before crossing a bridge, have a good look in front and behind you to see if there are any pack animals preparing to cross. Animals such as yaks can be easily spooked when crossing rickety bridges, and you will not want to be on the bridge at the same time. If you find yourself about to be passed by a pack animal on a trail, stand out of the way on the uphill side so that you cannot be knocked down the mountain.

Robbery And Theft

Although this usually occurs in towns and cities, it has been known for items to go missing whilst travelling through the mountains. Most theft is opportune and therefore avoidable; a trekker leaves an expensive-looking object lying around and somebody gives in to temptation. The chance of being robbed can be drastically reduced by:

- Minimising the amount of expensive gear carried or visibly displayed
- Depositing valuables in your hotel safe whilst staying in built-up areas
- Wearing inexpensive watches
- Leaving jewellery at home
- Appearing confident and being aware of people around you

'Whenever you pitch your tent for the night, think what might happen to it if the weather breaks and you are stuck for a week. Are you likely to be drowned in spindrift? Or wiped out by huge powder avalanches? Or buried alive?'

Stephen Venables

Rucksacks are straightforward to break into because they cannot be easily locked. It is also possible for a belt or strap to get torn off in transit. Placing your rucksack inside a lockable bag whilst it is being transported is one way to reduce the chances of damage occurring. If you are forced to put your naked rucksack into the hold of an aircraft or the roof of a bus, it is worth pulling all the straps down flush against the rucksack. The hip belt can be tied around the outside of the main compartment. Be sure to empty the contents of the side and top pockets. Knotting any fastening straps together will make the rucksack more difficult to open. Arriving in a country with a large rucksack and hand luggage can make you a slow-moving target for thieves: it will be obvious that you are carrying all of your valuables about your person. Neck and waist wallets are best hidden beneath a fleece jacket rather than just a light shirt. Keep the taxi fare in a pocket so that you don't have to reveal a wad of notes. Make sure you know where you are going to stay: avoid being seen opening a map or delving into a guidebook.

You will need to decide whether to carry cash, travellers cheques, or a mixture of both. If you opt for cheques, enquire as to how long it will take to have them replaced in the country you are visiting. Some countries now allow you to withdraw cash from banks or cashpoint machines in either US dollars or the local currency with a credit card. Certain nations seem to favour one particular brand of credit card over another, so it is worth taking more than one card with you. It might be worth carrying a wallet stuffed with a wad of low-denomination notes. If you are confronted by someone who threatens violence if you do not hand over your money, you can then volunteer this money bag, rather than the hidden one(s) containing all your large bills. It is unlikely that your attacker is going to stand around and count your cash. Occasionally, thieves might slash at bags and straps with knives in order to gain access to your belongings. If this sort of behaviour has been reported in the country you are visiting, then you might want to line or cover your bags and handles with chicken wire, which is usually sufficient to resist most blades. At least one manufacturer now produces a flexible wire cage for rucksacks.

If you do experience a robbery, make sure you visit the nearest police post at the earliest opportunity in order to report the incident. Whilst the chance of recovering your possessions might be very low, you will at least be able to procure a copy of your statement for insurance purposes.

Civil Unrest/Political Instability

Some mountainous regions are in countries that are politically unstable. Before you depart, investigate the political situation and take heed of advice proffered by organisations such as the Foreign and Commonwealth Office (FCO). The FCO are also able to explain what support British nationals can expect to receive from their nearest embassy in times of difficulty. Trekking and climbing in bandit country might sound exciting to some people, when in reality being taken hostage or having one's life threatened is a very sobering experience. Travelling in a group of four or more, and hiring a local guide, is one way to minimise the chance of being targeted. If you find that civil unrest breaks out whilst you are in-country, try and contact your embassy to make them aware of your presence. Maintain a low profile in order to avoid attracting unwanted attention. *Appendix A contains contact details for the FCO.*

ASSESSING THE RISKS TO YOU

Additional reports on potential and real hazards in the country you are visiting can be gained from recently published guidebooks, web sites, magazines and by talking to people who have just come from the destination. Having gathered all this information, you can then gauge whether the trip is reasonably safe to undertake. If you are aware of the potential risks posed to you, you will be much less likely to find yourself in trouble in the first place. During your journey it is worth continuing to seek the opinions of local people and visitors alike. Talking to other travellers when you arrive in-country is an excellent way of finding out what might lie in store for you. *A more formal approach to risk assessment is included in Chapter 12.*

YOUR QUESTIONS ANSWERED

I'm thinking of using an overnight bus service to get to the start of my trek. Is this a safe thing to do?

Bus garages are usually rich picking grounds for thieves. Don't leave your bags unattended – even for a moment – and have all valuables pre-packed in your carry-on luggage. You will need to be on your guard when you are at your lowest ebb; many travellers report having gear stolen moments after disembarking from all-night bus journeys.

However, the greatest danger is the journey itself. After heart attacks, road accidents are the leading cause of death amongst travellers. Driving at any time can be hazardous, but particularly so at night. If you want to significantly increase your margin of safety, travel during the day and make sure the journey finishes by dusk. When a night journey is unavoidable, you can increase your margin of safety by booking with a reputable bus company.

7

© Martin Hartley

> *Artists don't stint themselves with paper — nor should photographers stint themselves with film. Shoot, shoot and shoot again. Experiment and keep on experimenting. Analyse your pictures to learn what works and what doesn't.*
>
> *John Cleare*

Take Nothing But Photographs...

The mountain environment brings out the photographer in most people. Perhaps this is brought on by an urge to record the vistas for the folks back home. Or maybe it is a desire to capture your experiences in technicolour, rather than relying on memory (which invariably washes out to a sepia tint over time). On a commercial footing, members of an expedition may need images to illustrate a lecture or a magazine article. Meanwhile, the advent of palm-sized digital video cameras has encouraged an increasing number of mountain travellers to try their hand at the moving image game. The notes in this chapter are primarily for people wanting to get into mountain photography or video for the first time.

> *Always ask before taking photographs of people. Don't worry if you don't speak the language — a smile and a gesture will be understood and appreciated.*
>
> *Martin Hartley*

PHOTOGRAPHY

Film speeds, camera bodies, lenses, filters... all of this and more will need to be considered if you are planning to buy a camera and film — and that's before you've taken a single picture. *If you already own a camera and are*

> *Though the camera may be an expensive precision instrument, it is only a tool. It's the eye behind the camera that makes the picture.*
>
> John Cleare

happy with your choice of film but want to improve your photographic results, spin forward to 'Composing Your Picture' .

Which Type Of Film?

One of your first decisions will be to decide the medium you would like to receive your processed pictures on. The film that you choose will inevitably narrow down the choice of appropriate camera hardware. Give a lot of thought to the type of film that you want to use – there are several to choose from. They include:

35mm

35mm film remains the most popular film type for mountaineers and trekkers, despite the advent of other systems such as the Advanced Photo System.

Advanced Photo System (APS)

A modern, easy-to-load film. APS allows the photographer to switch between a number of views ('classic', 'panoramic', etc.) on the same roll of film.

Medium And Large Formats

These formats come in a range of sizes that all produce larger negatives than either 35mm or APS, making them ideal for professional photographers. Unsurprisingly, the cameras which use this film are large, heavy and expensive.

Print Or Slide Film?

When you are choosing the type of film, you will also have to choose whether you want to shoot print (negative) or slide (transparency) film. Print film is great if you want to show your friends where you have been. Print film is more likely to produce acceptable results in less expensive cameras that lack sophisticated light metering. Slide film is essential if you plan to give a lecture or submit images to a magazine. Slides can easily be turned into prints, but it is more difficult to do it the other way around. Before you buy your camera, make sure that the photographic film it uses is available in print or slide as you prefer. 35mm film is available in both formats.

What Film Speed?

All films have a speed rating. Films with a slow speed (typically 12 to 100 ASA/ISO) have a fine 'grain'. The finer the grain, the larger the picture can be enlarged without becoming fuzzy. However, films with slow speeds require more light to expose the picture correctly. Fast films (400 to 1600

ISO) have larger grains and need less light. These are ideal in low light
conditions or when shooting fast-moving objects as the picture can be taken
very quickly, with the shutter remaining open for only a few thousandths of
a second. Most climbers and trekkers discover that film speeds of between
50 and 200 ISO are ideal for mountain photography, with perhaps the odd
roll of 400 speed film for interior shots of buildings such as monasteries.

All Film Brands Are Not The Same

Once you have chosen the film type, you will need to choose a brand. If
you have time, fire off a roll or two of several different brands and check the
results for yourself. Bear in mind that the high mountain environment often
produces a different effect to that achieved in the lowlands.

How Much Film?

One answer is: as much as you can afford, and as much as you can carry. If
you are heading out on your first trek and are determined to capture the
entire experience on celluloid, a roll of film a day should be more than
sufficient. If you end up with too much unused film you can always use it
next time or sell it on to fellow travellers who have run out. Backpackers
and mountaineers who do not want to witness the entire journey through a
viewfinder the size of a postage stamp can easily get away with a couple of
rolls per week.

Thinking Of Going Digital?

The digital revolution in photographic cameras is yet to become popular with mountain travellers in the way that digital video has. There are two reasons for this. To begin with, in all but the top-end digital camera models, picture quality is not quite as good in digital as it is in conventional 35mm. Secondly, digital cameras require either a computer to download images on, or a stack of expensive memory cards. The advantages of digital are clear; you can view the picture immediately after taking it and either keep or discard the image, and there are no processing costs (although printing images out through a high-quality printer might prove costly).

Single Lens Reflex (SLR) Or Compact Camera?

If you opt for an APS or digital camera, then you are likely to end up buying a compact model, although some SLR cameras are available for both these formats. 35mm users go for either a SLR or a compact camera (or both).

A compact is literally that: a small point-and-shoot design that is sometimes small enough to slip into the breast pocket of a shirt. However the small size might mean that the operating buttons are very small, which could turn into a nightmare in cold weather if you are wearing gloves. Other compacts sport zoom lenses and weatherproof characteristics which increase their versatility, price and size. In low light conditions, compacts with long zooms might require the camera flash to fire in order to brighten up the subject sufficiently to take the picture: this might not result in the kind of image that you want to capture.

SLRs normally consist of a camera body and one or more interchangeable lenses. Heavier and more expensive than compact cameras, SLRs offer much more flexibility and remain the camera type of choice for the vast majority of photographic enthusiasts and professionals.

Whichever model you buy, take the time to shoot plenty of practice rolls on different settings in a number of environments – and in various lighting conditions – before departure to help you to get the best possible photographic results during your journey.

Lenses

Ask a professional photographer whether the optical quality of a lens is more important than the camera body and the answer is likely to be 'yes'. SLR lenses can be broken down into three principle groups: standard, wide-angle and telephoto.

Standard lenses (around 50mm) give approximately the same view as the human eye looking straight ahead. Most SLRs come with a 50mm lens as standard, and it can be a good lens to have as a back-up and for use in low light conditions as it is usually a relatively 'fast' lens. Photographers talk about fast and slow lenses all the time: a fast lens can be used in relatively low light conditions without recourse to a flash unit. The fastest lenses are very pricey. The good news is that there is normally lots of light around in the mountains. So a fast lens, whilst desirable, is by no means essential.

Wide-angle lenses (up to 35mm) are great in the mountains, as they take in a wide field-of-view. 24mm and 28mm are particularly popular.

Telephoto lenses (70mm and beyond) allow you to capture pictures of people and wildlife that are a long way away. Telephoto lenses are longer and heavier than other lenses. 135mm lenses can often be found in the bags of travel photographers. One low-cost way of extending the range of a telephoto lens is to fit it with a '2x' converter lens. This would turn a 150mm lens into a 300mm lens, albeit at the expense of a slight loss in optical quality.

Instead of purchasing two or three different lenses, many climbers and trekkers opt for one or two zoom lenses, such as a 24-50mm and a 70-210mm. With a zoom lens you can simply toggle the lens back and forth until the image you want to see is sitting in the viewfinder. The disadvantage of zoom lenses is that they are usually slower (that speed thing again!) but can often work out to be an acceptable compromise between weight, bulk, cost and efficiency.

Accessories

The experienced photographer leaves an ultra-violet (UV) or skylight filter screwed permanently to each lens to protect the glass from damage. After all, it is cheaper to replace a filter than a scratched lens. You might find it worthwhile to experiment with warming (81a) polarising (PL) and neutral density (ND) filters: most camera shops have little booklets (produced by the filter manufacturers) that show what effect different filters create. Mountain photographers tempted to experiment with other jazzy filters run the risk of turning a beautiful landscape into a scene from a sci-fi movie.

Full-size telescopic tripods are usually only carried by the most dedicated photographers. Miniature tripods weighing just a few grams can perform adequately if there is a nearby rock or wall to place them on. Alternatively, a monopod attachment can be screwed to a trekking pole.

*A camera's built-in light meter only records the light *reflected* from the subject, which can give an incorrect reading. A simple and effective way to get around this is to buy a handheld light meter, which measures the light that falls *onto* the subject. You simply transfer the exposure information from the meter to your camera and – voila, perfectly exposed photos every time.*

Steve Watkins

Another jaw-dropping vista for the photo album

If you plan to explore the dark world of night photography, invest in a cable release. This will allow you to press and hold the shutter open for seconds or minutes without touching the apparatus and so avoid 'camera shake' which is guaranteed to ruin your hard work.

PROTECTING YOUR CAMERA

Most mountaineers and trekkers use waterproofed, padded camera bags and clip these onto the waist belt or shoulder strap of their rucksacks. Make sure that the pouch you buy allows you to get your camera in and out easily. The harsh mountain environment is not ideal for sensitive camera equipment. The main problems include:

Fingers

Inevitably, fingerprints will appear on lenses and filters. This can lead to soft images. Cure: Use a proprietary cleaner in camp to return the surface of your lens to an 'as new' condition. During the day a microfibre cloth (bought from a specialist camera shop) will suffice.

Dust

Dust and grit can get into cameras and lenses, resulting in scratches and blemishes on processed pictures. Cure: Clean your equipment every day with a canister of compressed air before wiping with a cloth. (Check to make sure that this product does not violate airline regulations if you are flying to your destination.)

Cold Weather

Freezing temperatures can run down batteries and make film brittle. Cure: carry a spare set of batteries in a pocket close to the skin and rotate when

> ❝ I've stuck a few pieces of silver duct tape to my camera in order to make it look well-used and much less attractive to thieves. ❞
>
> *Martin Hartley*

necessary. Rewind film inside a warm sleeping bag at night. However, be aware that taking a camera from a cold to a warm environment can cause water vapour on the camera body and lens to condense. Wipe off this moisture before going back outside to prevent the camera from icing up.

High Altitude

The weight of most SLR systems often becomes unjustifiable above 6000m. Cure: swap the SLR in favour of two 35mm compact cameras that are worn inside windproof clothing. Two cameras will allow you to shoot up to 72 frames in a single day without needing to change films. A so-called 'disposable' camera can be a useful back-up for summit shots as it is inexpensive, lightweight and works in the very low temperatures associated with high altitude.

Humid Conditions

Humid conditions can cause condensation to form inside the camera. Cure: dry the camera by opening the back up and placing it inside a re-sealable bag with an anti-humidity sheet or a bag of silica.

Hot Temperatures

Heat can cause a change in colours on celluloid film. Cure: leave film in the shade whenever possible, but never in a sealed tent or car as temperatures in these environments can soar.

Water

Rain can damage and even destroy camera equipment. Cure: in wet weather, an SLR camera can be placed inside a clear plastic bag. A hole needs to be cut for the lens and this can be secured in place with a rubber band. If you are approaching the mountains by sea, a highly water-resistant or waterproof camera, or a watertight camera bag, is essential as cameras hate salt water.

> Cameras round the neck are a real pain when climbing, so I keep my compact camera to hand in a padded case attached to one side of my climbing harness. That way I get the shots that count, especially images taken in extreme situations.
>
> *Jerry Gore*

COMPOSING YOUR PICTURE

Practice makes perfect when taking photographs. Nevertheless, the following nuggets of information might help to get you off to a flying start.

Anticipation Is Everything

Being aware of what is going on and trying to anticipate events will give you the best chance of capturing the perfect shot. This might mean working out the best place from which to capture a sunrise, or travelling ahead of other members of the group to give yourself time to compose the picture.

Look Around The Camera's Viewfinder

Before you take a photograph, take time to look around inside the viewfinder. Some photographers imagine that they are looking into the room of a new house, and studying the walls and ceiling. By applying this concept to all four sides of the viewfinder, you will dramatically increase the chance of your subject being captured in its entirety.

Remember The 'Rule Of Thirds'

When taking photographs of landscapes, the rule of thirds suggests that the foreground dominates the bottom third, the centre ground is captured by the middle third, and the top third encapsulates the sky. Thirds work better than halves because they lead the viewer into the photograph, and provide 'time' to look around the picture.

Think About Scale

Many photographers who take pictures of landscapes simply can't explain to friends back home just how big the mountains are. Having a person or other identifiable object in a corner of the picture is one way to enable the viewer to appreciate the enormity of the surroundings.

Avoid Placing People In The Middle Of The Frame

It is usually better to have people standing or sitting to the left or right of centre. Also, remember that if people in your pictures are looking or walking out of the frame then they will lead the viewer to look away from your photograph.

The Best Shots Are Those You Least Want To Take

It's when you are cold and tired that some of the best potential photo opportunities come about. Always make the effort to take just one more shot, *especially* when you really can't be bothered to.

When You Get Home

Once you return with your undeveloped films, try to find a reliable lab that cares about your work. There's no point spending hundreds or even thousands of pounds on a trip, a camera and multitudinous rolls of film only to have the developers ruin the results. If you are unsure about the quality of a lab, why not process a single roll so that you can gauge the results? Once you get your images back, take time to archive your photos. Study the pictures and see what you want to improve next time you're out. If you want to enlarge some pictures to hang on the wall, remember that some photographs can be improved by cropping the image. Finally, choose an appropriate frame. Cheap 'clip frames' do little to enhance a photograph.

VIDEO

Before buying a video camcorder, it might be worth asking yourself exactly what you hope to achieve. There is an enormous difference between recording events on a trek and making a film. Dozens of components go into making a film, from shooting scenes and building sequences through to narrating, editing the results and adding a musical score. These notes are for the backpacker or mountaineer planning to use a consumer product (rather than a professional camcorder) to capture the essence of their venture either for personal pleasure or – at the most – to spice up a lecture about the experience.

Digital vs. Analogue

Digital camcorders are lighter and smaller than their analogue counterparts. Image quality from a digital camcorder is also noticeably higher. Nevertheless, a number of the older analogue formats are still available and the price of these has fallen dramatically. So if you are working on a budget but still want to record your mountain journey, an analogue machine could be worth looking at.

At all costs, avoid purchasing your video camcorder the week before you depart (the same can be said of photographic equipment). To begin with it might be faulty. Even if it works flawlessly, you will not have had sufficient time to become acquainted with its idiosyncrasies. Buying your camcorder several weeks or months before you depart will allow you to try it out on training weekends, see for yourself how long the batteries last and work out what all the buttons do.

With a lightweight
video camera, anyone can
try their hand at
recording

Features To Look For

Modern video camcorders are packed with features. Only a handful will
make a noticeable difference when filming in the mountains. These include:

External Battery

If the camcorder battery docks onto the outside of the video camcorder
(rather than inside the camcorder housing) then it is likely that you will be
able to augment the standard cell with one or more beefier batteries. These
are noticeably heavier than the original battery but may last up to four times
longer. If your cell lives inside the camcorder then the only practical way to
extend its running time will be to wire it up to a battery belt that is worn
around the waist or in the rucksack. The problem with a belt rig is that the
cable can become tangled up with other equipment. *Additional
information on batteries can be found in Chapter 14.*

Big Buttons

Camcorders the size of personal stereo cassette players may look great, but
can you operate the device in cold weather with your gloves on? There's
only one way to find out: take your gloves with you to the shop.

External Microphone Socket

Many film-makers claim that sound is more important than the pictures.

Sound can also be very difficult to capture faithfully. The built-in microphones on video camcorders are usually omni-directional, which means they will pick up noise from every direction, including the sound of the machine itself and the laboured breathing of the cameraman. A directional condenser microphone (with its own battery power supply) plugged into the camcorder and held out-of-shot, will faithfully record sounds and so bring a great deal of life to your footage. Small tie clip-on mikes are ideal for interviews. All mikes need wind hoods (known in the industry as 'Shaggy Dogs'). Hoods allow sounds to be captured, but filter out the wind which can otherwise play havoc with sound recordings.

Zoom Lens

You might find two types of zoom lens on digital camcorders: optical and electronic. The optical zoom is the 'true' zoom, whereas the electronic zoom is computer-manipulated to produce the best possible picture. For general shooting try and use only the optical zoom as this will produce a better quality image.

Manual Focus

Like SLR cameras, a manual over-ride is vital in certain circumstances, particularly when the camcorder has trouble focusing on the image (a common situation in low light conditions and when the subject is moving very quickly).

White Balance Facility

Small camcorders work better in low light than in bright conditions. Most models can still produce an image in an environment that is lit by a single candle (which is handy when filming in tents and snowholes); certain camcorders go so far as to have a 'night-vision' capability and electronically create their surrounding as a black-and-white picture even in total darkness.

When moving from a brightly-lit to a dimly-lit environment, it will probably be necessary to re-set the white balance on the camcorder so that people and landscapes are exposed correctly. A camcorder can do this automatically. However, a better result can be achieved by holding up a sheet of white paper in front of the camera and then manually re-setting the white balance facility.

Whilst a large semi professional camcorder is likely to be more robust and have the majority of these features, a smaller and lighter camcorder will probably be used more often, for the simple reason that it can be carried in a pocket and so be brought quickly to the eye.

'New technology has brought the possibility of making high quality adventure programmes to virtually anyone who wants to try. But the basics remain the same: a good story, told simply. A 10 minute video-short invariably packs more punch than 50 minutes of self-indulgence. Plan, plan and plan again!'

Jim Curran

> The aspiring
> filmmaker's
> most important
> piece of
> equipment is a
> pen and paper.
> If you can't
> write out your
> story on a
> piece of
> paper, you
> won't be able
> to even begin
> telling it on
> film.

Phil Coates

Recording Tips

The co-operation of the people around you is vital if you are to have any success with your recording. For example, from time-to-time you will probably need members of your group to re-enact certain scenes. When shooting people, record close-ups whenever possible, especially when the person is being interviewed or conducting a diary-style monologue straight to camcorder.

The professional cameraman rarely zooms in or out or pans from left to right whilst recording, as both effects can create a feeling of sea sickness amongst viewers. Instead, use the zoom to frame your shot and then allow the action to take place inside the viewfinder. Occasionally the zoom will be used whilst recording. For example, by practising with the zoom controls, you will be able to zoom out slowly and smoothly in order to hold an individual walking towards the camcorder in the frame.

By shooting sequences rather than single shots you will have more flexibility at the editing stage. Each shot might be recorded separately for up to 20 seconds, and edited down to seven to 10 seconds back at home. Another way to film the sequence – especially if you do not have access to editing facilities – is to 'shoot to edit': by filming the entire sequence in the correct order, the piece might be of a high enough standard to use in a lecture without further editing. If you decide to shoot to edit, the key to success is to plan in advance. Either approach will count for nothing if the 'actors' (a.k.a. the team members) look at the camcorder – unless they are being interviewed.

Essential Accessories

In addition to the camcorder, microphone and batteries, the following items are likely to prove useful: a skylight filter to protect the lens; a neutral density filter to improve picture quality in high contrast situations (such as a person walking across a snowfield on a bright day); a pan and tilt fluid head tripod; a monopod (if the weight of a tripod cannot be justified); and a silk or microfibre lens cloth. It's worth experimenting with different ways of connecting your padded camcorder bag to the outside of your rucksack or climbing harness so that it remains to hand. Always keep a spare battery and cassette to hand (the latter in a zip-lock bag).

Looking After Your Film

The experienced cameraman avoids opening his camcorder in a tent whilst the stove is on, in order to prevent condensation from forming inside the apparatus. Furthermore, he will resist the temptation to review what he has filmed on the built-in liquid-crystal display (LCD) in case any dirt and dust that has penetrated the machine's housing damages the tape during playback. (However, LCDs are great for framing shots before commencing a recording, and can also be used whilst filming, particularly if holding the camera low to the ground or when filming oneself: some screens can be rotated 180° for this purpose.) When choosing a camcorder, buy a model that has a secure tape-locking mechanism. This will reduce the amount of grit that can enter the machine.

YOUR QUESTIONS ANSWERED

What features should I look for in a new photographic camera?

The mountain traveller who is enthusiastic about his photography might find the following four features to be of particular interest. They are available on the majority of SLRs and also on some compact cameras.

Spot-metering
Allows you to take a light reading from a specific object. This can then determine the metering for the entire picture. Very useful in conditions of bright sunshine and on snow where people can be portrayed as silhouettes.

Fill-in flash
The mountaineer's friend. A fill-in flash option allows the camera's built-in flash to fire at a reduced level in order to artificially lighten a subject close to the lens. Ever wondered how climbers wearing hats or climbing helmets have been photographed with the sun behind them yet without their faces in shadow? Now you know.

Automatic bracketing
Auto-bracketing allows the camera to take three photographs of the same image all at different exposure readings. This can be handy if you think that the camera's built-in light meter might be fooled by the prevailing light. If the camera gets it wrong, this feature can help to put it right by virtue of the fact that at least one of three images is likely to be correctly exposed. This feature is particularly useful if you are using slide film.

Manual over-ride
The vast majority of SLRs and compact cameras have computer-controlled focusing, exposure and shutter speed. Left to its own devices, even the most modern SLR will behave just like an old-fashioned point-and-shoot instamatic, albeit a very sophisticated one. However, it is likely that there will be times when you will want some degree of creative control so it is worth making sure that the computer allows partial or full manual over-ride.

8

> ❝The wood used for heating and cooking in most Himalayan lodges still comes from non-sustainable sources, so if you use them you will contribute to the significant problem of tourism-related deforestation. If you think this is a bad thing then let lodge owners know that you would prefer to use accommodation that uses kerosene for fuel, even if it does cost a little more.❞
>
> *Tim Macartney-Snape*

...Leave Nothing But Footprints

As the number of backpackers and mountaineers increases year-on-year, the mountain environment is now being damaged by both tourists and the local people who attempt to accommodate their requests for housing, showers and bottled drinks. Rubbish, trail erosion, destruction of wildlife habitat and contamination of water sources are just some of the many abuses being inflicted. What can the individual mountain traveller do in order to minimise his environmental footprint? The answer is quite a lot, and it doesn't have to take much time or effort. Furthermore, an environmentally sensitive approach can actually save you money. This chapter highlights some of the things you might want to think about before and during your next mountain adventure.

AVOID POPULAR PLACES AT BUSY TIMES OF YEAR

The peak seasons on Kilimanjaro, the Everest trek, the Tour of Mont Blanc and the Inca Trail (to name but a few) can become depressingly busy. By visiting these places at the very start or end of the popular seasons you will almost certainly have a more enjoyable trip and at the same time help to take the pressure off the local environment. Flights and services can also be less expensive at these times of year. Better still, investigate other approaches to avoid the standard routes altogether. *Chapter 1 includes a table on the different times of year that these and other destinations can be visited.*

REMOVE EXTRANEOUS PACKAGING BEFORE DEPARTURE

Rubbish bins in mountainous regions discourage people from taking their litter with them and may be emptied only occasionally

Many products - from stove spares to chocolate biscuits - are sold with excessive amounts of packaging. Removing as much of this potential rubbish as possible before departure saves weight, and minimises the volume of rubbish to be dealt with in-country.

THINK ABOUT WHERE TO DEPOSIT YOUR RUBBISH

If you are on a commercial trek or expedition, your staff will usually offer to dispose of your rubbish. It is interesting to note that what they mean by disposal could be entirely different from your understanding of the word.

The majority of rubbish accrued in mountainous regions is either thrown down a nearby hillside, dumped in a river, burnt or buried. Scattering litter down the side of a hill creates a ghastly mess, and encourages vermin if it contains traces of food. Burning is no better, as it is almost impossible to completely incinerate all rubbish, especially glass, plastic and tin. Bonfires always leave behind ugly scars on the landscape, especially at altitude where any attempt to burn rubbish is likely to fail, on account of the rarefied atmosphere. Buried rubbish is often dug up by animals after an easy meal.

You might begin to wonder what *can* be done with your rubbish. There are a number of solutions. If you are travelling in a country that has facilities to deal with litter then try and hold onto your trash until you can personally deposit it in one of these places.

Another option is to carry your rubbish out of the mountains and take it to the nearest town or village. The problem with this approach is that human habitations in the mountains are themselves becoming over-polluted. One solution is to take home items like plastic wrappers that you brought out with you at the start of your journey.

NICK LEWIS' BIODEGRADABLE PLASTIC BAG POLICY

Get hold of a biodegradable plastic carrier bag – that really technical piece of equipment. Put it in your pocket or keep it in your rucksack. Whenever you see some rubbish on the trail, pick it up, put it in the bag and tie it to the outside of your rucksack. I've looked into this and discovered that the reason why people don't pick up rubbish is that they are afraid that they are going to get their rucksack or pocket dirty. If everyone picks up rubbish in this way we may encounter a little less litter on the trail.

TAKE YOUR BATTERIES HOME WITH YOU

A large number of climbers and trekkers bring fresh batteries from their own countries. Taking the dead cells home at the end of the trip guarantees that they will not leak into the mountain environment. Most developing countries have no facilities for dealing with used batteries.

AVOID BOTTLED WATER

A problem in almost every populated mountain environment is the disposal of empty plastic water bottles. Investing in water purification tablets or a pump will allow you to produce drinkable water from almost any water source. If trekkers stop buying bottled water in the mountains, local people will no longer carry it in to these places. When you think about it, importing water to glaciated mountain ranges is pretty daft. In some mountain villages, local environmental entrepreneurs are purifying water in heated, pressurised containers. *You can read about different methods of purifying water in Chapter 9.*

PROTECT WATER SUPPLIES

In addition to siting toilets away from water sources, make every effort to avoid contaminating the water with pollutants such as soap, regardless of whether the substance is environmentally-friendly or not. This can be achieved by filling a container with water, carrying it the appropriate distance away from the water source, washing yourself, clothes or vegetables in the container, and then pouring away the contaminated water. This might take a little longer than doing it all on the river bank, but guarantees that a person taking water from the same source a little further downstream will not get to drink your soap suds.

STEER CLEAR OF FIZZY DRINKS

Like bottled water, fizzy drinks are only carried into the mountains because tourists want them. Some drink manufacturers supply their products in glass bottles, which of course are recyclable. However, the cost of carrying the bottles back out of the mountain environment is so high that they are normally left in the hills. One estimate in the 1990s put the number of discarded glass bottles in a particular Himalayan region at over half a million. Likewise, alcohol. If you fancy a tipple, why not avail yourself of the local brew rather than an expensive bottle of imported beer?

QUIZ YOUR TOUR OPERATOR

When choosing a commercial operator, you might want to ask what its environmental policy is towards issues like dealing with the rubbish that is generated on trips, and whether you can see a copy of any such policy. It might also be useful to ask whether the operator encourages clients to take personal responsibility for things like their used batteries. Does the company issue adequate clothing, shelter and stoves to its staff in order to minimise their reliance on wood fires? Whilst on the trek or climb, you should feel at liberty to observe whether the company's environmental policy is enforced. If not, you might decide to write to the operator at the end of the holiday concerning this matter.

DEAL WITH YOUR OWN WASTE

Try to make use of existing toilet facilities even if they are in an unpleasant condition. If there are no such amenities in your vicinity, site temporary ablutions at least 75 metres away from all water sources. A deep pit is not always the most appropriate disposal method for human faeces. Often the 'active' layer of soil is just a few inches under the surface, in which case a shallow trench can be dug. Turfs may be lifted and then replaced when the camp is re-sited. In areas of hard or frozen soil, or rock, faeces can be smeared on rocks to air-dry. Hiding faeces under a rock does not encourage rapid decomposition, or allow air-drying to occur. Ironically, 'hiding' is the most popular - and yet most environmentally inappropriate - way of dealing with human waste. Toilet paper may be burnt, but only in locations where there is a zero fire risk. A modern alternative is to carry used paper out of the mountain environment in a re-sealable plastic bag.

PHOTOGRAPH RATHER THAN PRESS FLOWERS

In some parts of the world, picking flowers and collecting seeds is illegal. Elsewhere, guides and porters might not be familiar with the concept of 'Take only photographs, leave only footprints' so squat down to look at flowers that are pointed out by your guide. This tactic will prevent the flower being picked and presented to you.

CHOOSE ESTABLISHMENTS THAT USE SOLAR POWER OR KEROSENE

An increasing number of mountain lodges are investing in kerosene or solar panels to provide electricity and hot water for showers. Staying at these establishments (rather than hostels that continue to burn wood) is a clear way to show your support for such initiatives. It should be noted that in some hostels, wood is only used in the initial stage of lighting a fire. The flames are subsequently fed with dried animal droppings, an excellent eco-friendly fuel.

MINIMISE TRAIL EROSION

In order to help to minimise trail erosion, you might want to consider some of the following points:

- Sticking to the main path will help prevent the creation of countless smaller trails leading to the same destination.
- In muddy conditions, a few well-placed stepping stones could save the area either side of the existing trail from being turned into a quagmire.
- A decade or more of growth in some alpine flora can be destroyed by a single footprint: a little knowledge about plants will allow you to both appreciate and avoid damaging individual species.

> *Don't bury your base camp trash, as birds and animals will dig it up and spread it all over the place. Make provision for taking it away for proper, permanent disposal.*
>
> *Steve Bell*

- Take heed of trail signs and barriers that ask trekkers to use alternative routes. By doing so, you will be helping management teams to maintain the local environment.
- If you are planning to join a commercial trek or expedition, remember that a small party requires less staff and pack animals. This in turn minimises the number of feet and hooves that contribute to trail erosion.

VISIT NATIONAL PARK OFFICES

If you are visiting a park, preserve or designated wilderness region it is possible that it might have its own team of wardens. These people are often well-informed about the local mountain environment and may be able to offer specific advice on a variety of topics including: where to dispose of litter; which plants are particularly susceptible to damage; and the condition of any marked trails. In the absence of any such administration, you might be able to pick up useful information from recently-published guidebooks to the area.

CHOOSE ENVIRONMENTALLY-FRIENDLY CLOTHING

The overwhelming majority of items found in outdoor stores begin life in the petrochemical industry; waterproof fabrics, pile clothing, sleeping bag covers, compasses... the list is endless. However, at least one material – fleece – can be made by recycling and re-processing plastic bottles. A recycled fleece pullover can be manufactured from about 25 two-litre bottles that would otherwise end up in a landfill site. This manufacturing process also avoids the consumption of oil and the creation of toxic air emissions that result from the production of 'virgin' fleece products. The same pollution argument can be applied to conventionally-grown cotton; a kilo of non-organic cotton requires up to three kilos of pesticides and other pollutants to be used in its production. Organic cotton avoids this costly polluting process.

When there is no choice but to buy products made from 'virgin' materials, purchasing the most durable products that you can afford means that it could be a very long time indeed before the item wears out and needs to be replaced. This is good not only for rubbish dumps but your wallet too, as buying cheap often means buying twice.

Another cost-cutting measure is to extend the life of certain items of gear. This can be achieved by careful storage, judicious cleaning and professional repair. An excellent example is the down sleeping bag. Keeping a down bag fully lofted when not in use will maximise its useful life. Professionally wet-cleaning a dirty down bag costs a fraction of the price of a new bag, but will resurrect even the most tired pit into a warm and usable product once again. The same down bag can be re-shelled when the nylon outer wears thin. At this stage more down can be added in order to up-rate the bag's overall performance. In much the same way, jackets can be re-proofed, boots can be re-soled and rucksacks can be patched. When finally the item (to your eyes at least) needs replacing, it can be given to a member of local staff on your next trek, whereupon it will enjoy a whole new lease of life.

By contrast, personal protective equipment such as helmets, ropes and climbing harnesses should be discarded if they become damaged or when they approach the end of their serviceable life.

A local environmental initiative

GOING A LITTLE FURTHER

If you have read this far, then it is likely that you have a strong interest in preserving the mountain environment. There are a number of other ways that individuals can minimise their environmental footprints. People often come up with their own solutions after considering some of the questions posed by certain environmentalists. For example, what would Britain's reaction be to tens of thousands of visitors descending upon the English Lake District every summer, if they left the hills covered in rubbish and faeces in much the same way as countless westerners have done in parts of the Himalaya for the last 50 years?

If you are on a commercial trek, you might choose to lead by example when it comes to things like dealing with sweet wrappers. Being seen to collect all your rubbish and take it home may have a positive effect on both your staff and the other trekkers in your group. There can also be a temptation for staff to burn plastic and foil when the tourists' backs are turned, or to dump rubbish (that is being carried on a pack animal) at the top of a pass after the clients have begun descending the other side.

Getting involved and talking things through with your group leader may prove difficult; on the other hand an increasing number of mountain people are becoming more aware of the need to keep their hills free of pollution in order to ensure that tourists continue to visit. If clients, tour operators and trek leaders talk to each other about such situations, then it is more likely that practical solutions to these problems will be found.

Furthermore, if climbers and trekkers only sign up with operators that have effective environmental policies, then the companies that do not have this type of scheme will either go out of business or be forced to fall in line. However, visitors must be prepared to pay a little more so that companies are able to put policies into practice.

ADDITIONAL CONSIDERATIONS FOR GROUPS

As an increasing number of parties head for remote and popular mountain regions alike, it is becoming even more important for teams to avoid having an unnecessary impact on the environment. These points are for group leaders as well as individual trekkers who want to learn more about how responsible operators implement their environmental policy.

The principle consideration to bear in mind is that the number of members in your party will heavily influence the overall environmental impact of your expedition. Every member of the team contributes to:

- An increase in equipment, packaging and potential rubbish
- An escalation in the numbers of porters and cooks required
- Erosion at campsites and on the trail
- Fuel-polluting wheeled or winged transport
- A higher overall cost

By contrast, a small team which is committed to minimising its collective environmental 'footprint' can be highly successful from an ecological perspective. One of the methods that a group can use to calculate the

damage it is likely to inflict on the environment
(and thereby work out ways to reduce the
overall effect of its presence) is to draw up an
environmental policy that takes into account
the following suggestions.

Think About How Many Local Staff Are Needed

At some point a decision will have to be made
as to how many local people need to be
employed by the expedition. A team whose
members are prepared to carry more
equipment themselves will reduce the number
of porters and pack animals that need to be
hired. This approach saves money and reduces
the overall environmental impact of the
expedition.

Reduce Any Reliance On Single-Use Batteries

An increase in the use of battery-operated
devices (such as video cameras and GPS

Burning rubbish at
altitude is best avoided

receivers) by expeditions has led to a greater demand for power sources.
Fortunately, many mountain areas enjoy periodic bouts of bright sunshine
Lightweight, portable solar cells are ideal for recharging batteries. Larger
expeditions have experimented with a number of other environmentally-
friendly sources of power including wind machines. It is worth
remembering that at high altitude, conventional liquid fuel generators
perform poorly.

Investigate In-Country Conservation Measures And National Park Regulations

A large number of mountain environments have either notional or
rigorously-enforced environmental policies. The existence of such policies
needs to be determined during the planning phase of your expedition.
Where such regulations do not exist, your own environmental policy
becomes even more important.

Find Out About Existing Environmental Problems

Try to find out what environmental problems are already present in the area
that you plan to visit. This information can often be gleaned from:

- The news pages of specialist outdoor or environmental magazines
- Reports, guidebooks and articles
- Directly from friends, contacts and past expedition leaders who have visited the area

Not only will such information assist you in the design and implementation of your policy, it may also encourage you to make some effort to deal with the existing situation.

Decide Upon The Final Destination For Your Rubbish

Historically, expeditions have always dealt with their waste in-situ. For example, rubbish would be burnt at camps, thrown into crevasses or poured down a hillside. One modern approach for expeditions has been to take out all rubbish at the end of the climb.

Nevertheless, this new strategy is now spawning a problem of its own. So-called 'gateways' to the mountains (such as Gilgit in Pakistan) are now being forced to deal with vast quantities of rubbish that have been carried out by environmentally sensitive mountain travellers. The vast majority of these gateways have no recycling or processing facilities of any kind. As a result, expeditions are now being asked to consider the most appropriate final destination for their rubbish.

To aid this decision-making process, rubbish can be physically divided into four categories:

By providing porters with stoves and shelter, the use of wood fires like this one can be minimised

Burnable

Food leftovers, paper, card and wood can all be burnt at the end of the expedition when it returns to a low altitude. Ensure that a sufficient amount of liquid fuel is used to complete the burning process as thoroughly as possible. Burning can create an ugly scarring of the landscape and/or quickly rage out of control, so give due consideration to the location of your fire. One word of caution: if you do choose to burn your waste paper, enquire as to whether the hearth has a religious significance. In some cultures, fires are sacrosanct.

Non-burnable

Metals, gas canisters, plastics and foam can be given to local staff where such items serve a practical purpose, perhaps in the home. In some countries, gas canisters are re-filled by expedition companies as a matter of course. Otherwise, non-burnables should be physically taken to the nearest recycling or processing centre, which might well be in the home country.

Toxic

Liquid fuel, sanitary towels and medical waste must be disposed of sensitively. Some hospitals in towns or cities may be prepared to deal with medical waste. Excess fuel can be given to local staff for use in their homes or on future expeditions.

Human

On some mountains (such as Denali in Alaska and Vinson in Antarctica) a policy of removing human waste is rigorously enforced.

Consider Repatriation

An increasing number of expeditions are returning home with the waste generated from supplies originally brought out from their own countries. For teams travelling in many developing countries, this policy is the only viable means of disposal for certain items of rubbish. Many groups secure excess baggage allowances on their outward journey and are likely to be granted a similar allowance on their return. As a minimum, all individuals should attempt to bring back any personal rubbish (including plastic sweet wrappers) as well as items such as used batteries.

Discretion is often required when repatriating waste as there are strict regulations for transporting such material by air. Items such as clean food wrappers and used batteries may not present significant problems when transported in limited amounts, providing they are packaged properly prior to transportation. However, waste that has been contaminated with substances such as fuel or sewage will need special attention in order that it complies with national and international regulations, and this may have financial implications.

Involve Your Staff And Other Local People

You will need the co-operation of local people and your local staff in order to minimise the overall environmental footprint of the expedition. It is vital that time is taken to explain and demonstrate to local people the benefits to them of keeping base camp areas clean, water sources unpolluted and hillsides free of rubbish. A reduction in the amount of financial income received from tourists as a result of environmental damage, and contamination of village water supplies leading to sickness amongst the inhabitants, are just two examples of the direct and indirect ways that indigenous people can suffer if they do not help to maintain their local environment.

Leave Campsites As You Find Them

Campsites – be they for one or more nights – need to be chosen with respect to local flora and fauna. Rocks and other protrusions should be left in-situ, or put back in position when striking camp. Where a campsite has not been previously established, consider dispersing tents over a wide area.

Remove Other Rubbish

It is a sad fact that many expeditions come across other teams' rubbish. If possible, efforts should be made to remove this waste along with your own. If the rubbish can be photographed or otherwise identified, do so. This is easier in remote regions that receive few visits than in popular areas that absorb dozens of expeditions each year.

On the odd occasion that it proves impossible to remove all trace of your own expedition (e.g. emergency aeromedical evacuation) then all rubbish should be bagged and tagged, and attempts made to co-ordinate with future parties to remove the abandoned waste. If everyone aims to leave their campsite and route a little cleaner than it was found on arrival, the problem of waste from previous expeditions will lessen over time.

Publish The Environmental Report

A full report of the expedition's environmental policy – including all successes and failures – will help future teams when drawing up their own policies. However, with the number of pristine wilderness environments steadily declining, some mountaineers who do not apply for grants that require them to submit an expedition report are questioning whether accounts of their expeditions – be they official reports or articles for the general public – are better off not being written, in order to avoid drawing attention to unspoilt mountain areas.

YOUR QUESTIONS ANSWERED

We don't leave that much rubbish behind. Do we?

In many mountain regions it is difficult to measure just how much rubbish is being deposited. However, certain organisations such as Nepal's Sagarmartha Pollution Control Committee (SPCC), who work on the southern approaches to Everest Base Camp, are calculating the amount of refuse they collect. In 1993/94 they collected 126 metric tons of garbage. This had increased to 243 metric tons in 1996/97. It is estimated that there is 17 metric tons of garbage per kilometre of tourist trail in the Everest area alone. And of course that's just one mountain region in one mountain range.

9

© Martin Hartley

> *The rule of thumb in the mountains is: eat and drink the maximum whenever you can and you will be OK.*
>
> *Peter Hillary*

Eating And Drinking

Dreams of reaching summits, completing treks and traversing mountain ranges are turned into reality not just with detailed planning and preparation, but also by drinking adequate amounts of fluid and eating sufficient quantities of food.

FLUIDS

A regular and plentiful water supply is vital in order for your body to properly regulate its temperature and remain hydrated. It is almost impossible to drink too much when you are in the mountains.

Obtaining Enough To Drink

Increasing your fluid intake in the 24 hours before an important mountain day will ensure that you set off fully hydrated. In an ideal world, you would aim to drink at least every hour whilst trekking or climbing, but whether this can be achieved will depend upon several factors including the type of mountain activity you are engaged in, how much water you can carry and how often you are able to refill your water bottle(s). It is vital to continue rehydrating at the end of the day's activities. Alcohol and drinks that contain

> *Remember that your muscles and joints depend on a good fluid intake, so always drink plenty of plain water at regular intervals during the day.*
>
> *Vivian Grisogono*

caffeine don't count as they only serve to increase the amount of water you lose in your urine.

If you try to tough it out without drinking, your physical and mental performance will nose-dive. Medical conditions such as heat exhaustion are a direct consequence of dehydration. By making an effort to include drinking as part of your routine, you will be less likely to forget to drink when it is really important.

However, water consumption is only half the battle. The 'invisible' fight is to get the body to actually absorb the consumed water. Sipping plain cold water can be very effective but adding a pinch of salt and some carbohydrate (e.g. from fruit juice or squash) can improve the body's ability to absorb the fluid. You can make up these mixtures yourself, or purchase a proprietary sports drink product which contains the correct amounts of salt and glucose polymers.

Carrying Enough To Drink

On most mountain treks it is useful to be able to carry a minimum of two litres. This might be in the form of a single large bottle or two or more smaller containers. Most bottles are made from either lacquered aluminium, hard plastic, flexible nylon or collapsible plastic. The most important thing is that the one you choose doesn't leak! Cheap bottles often drip when they are turned upside-down. Some containers now come equipped with flexible hoses, which allow you to sip water little and often. This is widely regarded as being the most effective way to remain hydrated.

Some backpackers and mountaineers on organised trips complain that they are unable to obtain enough drinking water from their cook team. Whilst fuel and time restrictions may prevent the staff from producing several litres of boiled water per day for every person, if you are carrying your own water treatment then you will be able to go to the water source and collect extra fluid.

Making Water Safe To Drink

Water must be purified in order to make it safe to drink. Purification is a two-stage process that requires the water to be clarified and sterilised. It is a good idea to carry two methods of treating water (even if they are identical) in case one is lost or broken.

Clarification involves removing obvious contaminants from the water, such as dirt, glacial till, leaves and other rubbish. Ideally, your chosen water

source will be one that is already free from obvious contaminants; a spring, fast-flowing stream or a tap are ideal sources of clarified water. Take a few moments to check that your water source isn't downstream from a village, campsite or a regular drinking place for animals. If you are forced to take your water from an unclarified source (such as a lake) then much can be done to improve the quality of the water. For example, it can be passed through a succession of fine muslin screens. Alternatively, the water can be poured into a tightly-woven canvas pouch known as a 'Millbank Bag'. If you find yourself needing to clarify water but have no equipment to do so, a sock filled with clean sand may suffice. Simply pour the water in the top and collect the clarified water that drips out of the toe end. Replace the sand after each use. Water can also be left to stand in a container for a period of time to allow silt to sink to the bottom of the container.

Clarified water needs to be sterilised. Sterilisation involves killing all the contaminants that you cannot see with the naked eye – including bacteria and viruses – as well as single-cell parasites and their spores. This is normally achieved by treating the water with a chemical. Whilst tablets containing silver can be used for long-term water treatment (silver helps to prevent re-contamination) iodine is the most effective chemical to make water drinkable on a day-to-day basis. Commercially-available iodine for the purpose of sterilising water is available from many outdoor stores in the form of droplets and tablets. If the water you are treating is very cold, the standard dosage and treatment time indicated on the side of the product may need to be increased in order to ensure that all infectious agents – including Giardia cysts – are eliminated. Whilst a 45-minute treatment time for iodine is generally regarded as appropriate for treating cold mountain stream water, a period of two hours might be necessary for absolute effectiveness. In practice, it might not always be possible to wait this length of time, although treating dubious or very cold water overnight is one way to ensure sterilisation. Be aware that if you buy iodine in a developing country, it might have a different level of potency from the liquid sold in the UK: ask for iodine tincture 2% in alcohol.

Some people who work in the field of water purification have said that iodine used exclusively over a long period of time (the actual length varies from individual-to-individual) can cause health problems. However, for the majority of mountain travellers who alternate iodine treatment with quantities of boiled tea and the occasional fizzy drink, iodine will prove to be a low-cost, effective means of water treatment. Individuals with thyroid disease should consult their doctor before using iodine.

One alternative to iodine is chlorine, which is effective providing that the dose (sold in tablet form) is strong enough. Be aware that the dosage instructions sold on the side of many packets of chlorine tablets are for use in places like the UK. Enquire before increasing the dose.

If you find the taste of iodine unpleasant then try treating your water the night before you need to drink it; by morning, the taint will be minimal. Any remaining iodine can be neutralised with Vitamin C (Ascorbic Acid). If you decide to do this, about a match-head of Vitamin C powder will neutralise one litre – any more than this and the water will taste worse than the iodine. If you decide to use this neutralisation treatment, it is vital that the Vitamin C is added *after* the iodine has been given sufficient time to treat the water. Also bear in mind that Vitamin C can leach into a plastic bottle, making any future iodine treatments less effective. The solution is either to use two plastic water bottles (one for the iodine and one for the Vitamin C) or a single lacquered aluminium bottle, as the Vitamin C cannot be absorbed by this type of container.

Pumps

Some trekkers and climbers prefer to use a water filtration or purification pump as a complete or partial replacement for the two-stage purification process.

Most pumps consist of: an inlet hose, which is placed in the water that is awaiting treatment; a hand-operated mechanism which forces the water through the internal filtering device; and an outlet spout or hose.

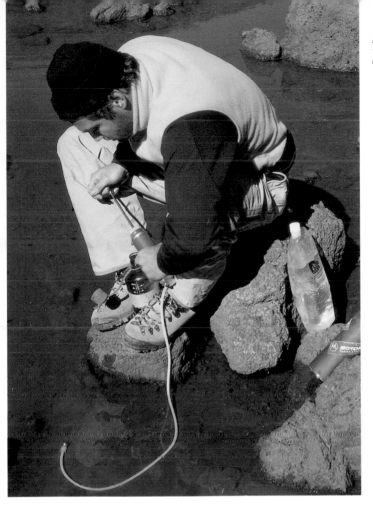

A water filter is one way
to provide safe, clean
drinking water

Pumps generally fall into one of two categories: 'filters' which claim to
remove contamination from the water by forcing the liquid through a
ceramic or similar candle; and 'purifiers' which additionally claim to treat the
water chemically. The disadvantage with all pumps is that eventually the
rubbish removed in the clarification process blocks them up. Some filtering
units can be easily dismantled, scrubbed clean and re-assembled. Others
must be replaced. The life of the pump can be extended by attaching a large
cork to the end of the inlet hose. The cork will encourage the hose to float
in order to allow the clearer liquid normally found near the surface of the
water source to be sucked up, as opposed to the crud that lies on the
bottom. One or more pre-filtering devices (such as the Millbank bag
described earlier) may also be used to prevent obviously dirty water
clogging up the pump.

It's worth trying out the different pumping mechanisms before you buy. Some handles require a downward force which can prove to be more tiring than attachments which allow the handle and unit to be driven together like a set of bellows.

Some backpackers prefer to treat the water with iodine tablets or droplets rather than rely on a purifier. If you plan to use a pump and a separate chemical treatment, be sure to pass the water through the pump first.

Boiling

A rolling boil for several minutes will also render water safe to drink. However, boiling becomes less effective at altitude: for every 300m of height gain above sea level, water boils 1°C lower. That might not sound like much, but at 4500m, water will boil at just 85°C which may be insufficient to kill all micro-organisms. In a moderate or high altitude situation, it is important to allow the water to boil for an additional four minutes to compensate for every 1000m of altitude. (You'll want to factor in the extra fuel needed to achieve this rolling boil). If you are staying in a hostel or tea house, you may have no choice but to rely on your host's word that the water has been properly boiled, rather than simply brought to boiling point.

Other Sources Of Contamination

If you are in a town and order a bottle of water or a can of fizzy pop, make sure that it is opened in front of you. Having gone to all this trouble, it would be unfortunate to have potentially contaminated ice cubes added to your drink. It is perhaps wise to treat all fruit juices and ice cream with caution, as many brands contain untreated water. Tap water should also be treated with great suspicion, even if all you want to do with it is wash vegetables and clean teeth. If you go to the trouble of checking that every drop of liquid that passes your lips has been purified to the best of your ability, you will have already gone a long way to ensuring that you remain healthy during your trip.

EATING WELL

In addition to drinking enough water, it is also essential to eat sufficient quantities of the correct foodstuffs whilst climbing and trekking. An adequate calorific intake will allow you to:

- Stay alert (thus reducing the risk of making mistakes due to exhaustion)
- Keep going for longer during the day

- Minimise the number of rest stops
- Be in a better position to continue the following day

A plentiful supply of food is not as critical as adequate hydration. That said, food becomes increasingly important as you approach the limits of your physical ability. Altitude and exercise both depress your appetite, yet the energy demands of mountain sports are high: you could end up needing more than twice as much energy as usual. However, long and demanding routes (especially when you are carrying all your own supplies) can make it difficult to eat sufficient quantities of food. The following advice has been written with both trekkers and mountaineers in mind.

- Take food that you really like. It's no good having nutritionally balanced food if you can't face eating it. Pack a variety of products as even your favourite snack can become boring.
- Whilst ideally 60-70% of your energy will come from the carbohydrate in your food, the foodstuffs will need to be items that can be easily carried, cooked and eaten.
- Plan food into the day. Mountaineers could agree in advance on which belay to take time out to eat. Backpackers might decide to have two shorter eating stops rather than one long lunch break.
- Fat adds palatability to food. This is a bonus, especially at altitude. But food with a high fat content is more likely to cause stomach discomfort.

Fresh food bought from a market can provide a welcome respite from packet meals

- During the day, snacks are better than big meals. Try to eat 20-60g of carbohydrate every hour. Eating small amounts of food regularly reduces the risk of indigestion when you eat at the end of the day.
- Fear and anxiety increase acid production in the stomach: food can help to protect the stomach lining.

Food In The Mountains

On some mountain journeys it will be necessary to eat dehydrated, freeze-dried and other lightweight foodstuffs for at least part of the trip. These can be found on the shelves of specialist outdoor stores and high street supermarkets. It is worth noting that the capital cities of many developing countries have at least one or two stores stocked with imported western foodstuffs. These shops are normally frequented by the local expatriate community. Discovering the location of one of these stores may save you from having to bring any food with you from your own country.

Nevertheless, eat fresh foodstuffs whenever you can. Indeed, if you are travelling independently and passing through villages, it may sometimes prove somewhat easier to obtain fresh rather than packaged foods. Make sure that all members of the group are willing to eat the food that is taken.

Packing Your Food

Give some thought to different ways to pack and store the food during your mountain journey. Fresh food can spoil quickly and plastic bags may easily split open. Many foodstuffs crush under the lightest pressure. Here are some ways to ensure that your oats don't become mixed with your onions:

Remove Excess Packaging

Some foodstuffs come with no less than three separate wrappings - outer cardboard box, inner cellophane and base plastic tray. Eliminating as much of this superfluous packaging as possible before departure saves weight and reduces the amount of rubbish to be carried out at the end of the trip.

Certain foodstuffs are better off being transferred into re-usable plastic containers. Miniature leakproof pots can be used for cooking oils, washing up liquid and spices. If you buy staple foods such as rice and potatoes in-country then remember that cotton sacks will last longer than plastic bags, and can be re-used by your staff at the end of your adventure.

Store Food In Animal-Proof Containers

Insects, vermin, birds and some much larger creatures such as bears all like the taste of human food. So research your intended destination to find out what animals are likely to be interested in your provisions and the best way to keep it out of reach.

Divide Food Into Ration Packs

Bagging food up before departure saves time during the trip. This policy also reduces the chance of every gram of one particular foodstuff being spoilt in transit. Losing all your energy bars at the start of a trip would be more difficult to deal with than having several 24-hour ration packs destroyed. Incidentally, the ration pack bags can be re-utilised as rubbish containers.

Keep All Foodstuffs Away From Fuel

Tiny quantities of paraffin can contaminate entire boxes of chocolate. If pack animals are being used, ensure that fuel and food do not travel on the same beast. This is important because if a load is thrown, the herder may gather up the spilt items and lash the fuel and food together. Fuel should also be kept well away from personal protective equipment such as helmets and ropes.

Bear in mind that cheap, locally-made plastic containers are often less robust than they appear – look inside the lid to see if a rubber seal is in place and then test before using.

'It is important to keep both body and spirits in good shape by eating and taking short rests regularly. It is easy to get demoralised and lose your nerve if you are exhausted.'

Tim Salmon

AVOIDING FOOD POISONING

Poorly-prepared or contaminated foodstuffs can quickly cause a gastrointestinal infection (commonly known as 'food poisoning') in even the well-seasoned traveller. If you order hot food, make sure that it is piping hot when it arrives on your plate. Similarly, chilled dishes are best consumed whilst they are still cold. You might want to avoid eating raw leafy vegetables, raw and room-temperature meats, raw fish and shellfish. Fruits are safe to eat only when they have been peeled. One final tip: decline milk and all milk by-products (such as cheese) unless they have been cooked or pasteurised.

Taking all these precautions might not leave you with much to eat! Furthermore, you might offend your host by turning down food, especially if a family has gone without in order to provide for you. It is up to the individual to weigh up the benefits of indulging in certain foods, against the unpleasantness caused by food poisoning. *You can read about how to treat diarrhoea in Chapter 5.*

FLUID AND FOOD REQUIREMENTS ABOVE 5000M

At altitudes above 5000m it may prove increasingly difficult (but not necessarily impossible) to find sources of running water. If none can be found then it will be necessary to melt snow and ice. It may take up to an hour to produce a single litre of water, and another 60 minutes to bring it to the boil. Unsurprisingly, it can be very tempting not to bother to have that vital extra hot drink in the morning.

However, consuming an adequate amount of liquid can make all the difference between summitting and turning back so do everything you can to force down as much water as possible. The actual amount of water you need to consume will depend on the altitude, the amount being carried, how many hours you are climbing for and how difficult the route is: wading through waist-deep snow will be far more laborious than walking atop a frozen surface. At altitudes above 5000m it will often prove impossible to produce and drink the four or more litres you need every day and this will inevitably have a detrimental effect on your mental and physical performance.

Nevertheless, there are ways of producing an adequate amount of water at altitude. For instance, you might find yourself having to choose between sleeping and brewing. In this type of situation many experienced mountaineers choose to keep the stove alight. During the day, climbing parties of three have found that whilst the first person climbs and the second belays, the third can melt water and fill water bottles. Another tip: by starting your ascent sufficiently early and finishing before 3pm, you will create a window of opportunity to brew up in the relative warmth of the late afternoon. As well as being more pleasurable than cooking in sub-zero temperatures, boiling water in the heat of the day also uses less fuel.

On glacial terrain, fuel is not always necessary to produce liquid. If you expect to operate from a fixed camp, why not include a 40-litre black, waterproof, canoe storage bag in your kit? On the walk-in, this can be used as a container for your spare clothing and sleeping bag. On arrival at the high camp, remove your kit from the bag and fill it with ice or snow. Leave the sealed bag inside the tent. Temperatures in a tent can sky-rocket during the day, resulting in a mushy or melted bag of snow for you to treat and drink on your return. The same tactic can be used on a much smaller scale by periodically topping up your water bottle with ice during the day. The most useful water bottles are made from non-reflective materials. These can be laid out during rest breaks to absorb the sun's rays. Flexible water bladders made from black materials are particularly effective in this regard.

Melting sufficient water is one difficulty to overcome;

preventing it from re-freezing is quite another. Insulated flasks may be used but they are usually too heavy. Furthermore, their effectiveness in cold temperatures usually falls well short of the manufacturer's claims. Some climbers pop their bottles inside down-filled booties but even this precaution only delays freezing for an hour or so. One sure-fire way to prevent your water from becoming frozen is to wear it inside your clothing, although carrying it in this manner can prove somewhat uncomfortable. People who attach a flexible hose to their water bottle will need to ensure that any remaining water in the tube does not freeze; blowing excess water back into the bottle after drinking helps.

Some people discover that their appetite declines sharply at high altitudes, whilst others find certain foodstuffs simply unpalatable. If sufficient calories are not forthcoming then the body will begin to cannibalise its own muscle and body fat. Generating sufficient enthusiasm to eat can be helped by packing a variety of your favourite foods. Furthermore, pickles, sauces and spices can help to enliven bland potato, rice and noodle dishes. Liquid foods (such as soup) are usually popular, as are hydrated meals in foil pouches. The latter are heavier than freeze-dried and dehydrated fare and can contain surprisingly few calories. On the other hand, they only require heating through and are less likely to leave you feeling thirsty (a common side-effect of dehydrated food). Whole milk powder can be added to many drinks and foods, and is an easy way to increase your protein and calorie intake. In cold weather, snack food is best carried in a pocket close to the body so that it remains soft enough to eat: cracking a tooth on a frozen bar of chocolate is a decidedly unpleasant experience. As more height is gained, red blood cell production increases. This places extra demands on the body's nutritional reserves. Some mountain travellers take vitamin and mineral supplements in tablet form. *Chapter 10 contains additional information on travel above 5000m.*

COOKING

If you have the opportunity before departure to cook the meals you intend to eat, you will be able to experiment with extra flavourings without spoiling the food when it really counts.

Camping in fine weather will allow you to cook al fresco. However, in wet conditions, many backpackers are forced to cook in their tent vestibule, even though this is heavily discouraged by tent manufacturers. Tents are highly flammable, and the consequences of a burning tent – especially if the incumbents are in their sleeping bags at the time of the blaze – could be disastrous. If you have no option but to cook inside the porch entrance, do not allow any part of the shelter to come anywhere near the stove.

Having the correct
equipment to be able to
cook your own meals will
increase your level of
independence in the
mountains

Be prepared to boot the entire stove away from the tent if the burner flares. If your tent does not have a rear exit, keep a knife handy so that you can slash and escape if the tent starts to burn. Familiarisation with the stove's operation will minimise the chance of the burner becoming uncontrollable during the lighting or cooking process.

If the stove's fuel tank needs refilling whilst you are cooking, turn off the burner and double-check that the flames have been properly extinguished before attempting to refill the tank. This is particularly important for stoves that burn transparent fuels, which produce a colourless flame.

All stoves give off carbon monoxide. A build-up of carbon monoxide in a confined area (such as a tent, snowhole or mountain hut) is undetectable without specialist equipment, and can rapidly lead to unconsciousness and death. For safety's sake, always ensure that you cook in a well-ventilated area.

Cooking In Winter Conditions

Cooking when there is snow on the ground, or when the temperature falls below freezing, requires some additional precautions. Firstly, it is important to prevent your fuel supply from solidifying. Gas cannisters can be popped in a sleeping bag half an hour before being connected to the stove, whilst a pressurised liquid fuel burner may need extra encouragement if regular priming is ineffective. This can be done by applying a small amount of 'burning paste' around the base of the stove. Light this paste, and allow the flames produced to heat the stove. When they have self-extinguished, open the fuel valve and ignite the burner.

A light dusting of snow can be brushed away before setting the stove down on frozen ground. However, if you are camping on a glacier, or on snow that is feet deep, it is imperative that a piece of insulating material is placed between the stove and the snow. If this precaution is not taken, your burner is likely to melt itself into the ice. If you are planning to camp on snow, consider packing something to act as a base. If you need to improvise, then a spare pan lid might suffice.

If you are forced to use snow or ice as your water source, then remember that ice produces a greater return, as it does not contain any air. If you only have snow available, it is worth taking the time to produce a pyramid of snowballs before starting to cook. Melting one snowball at a time is more efficient than filling a pan with snow.

YOUR QUESTIONS ANSWERED

Why doesn't my stove boil water as quickly as is stated in the specification sheet?

Some manufacturers test their stoves under favourable conditions, with no wind effect and using high-grade fuel. It is almost impossible to recreate this environment in the mountains. Nevertheless, there is much that can be done to reduce boiling times. Make sure that the cooking pan you buy comes with a well-fitting lid, as heating water in a covered container is an easy way to reduce boiling times and fuel consumption. In addition to insulating your stove and fuel bottle from the cold ground, a lightweight wraparound aluminium windshield that envelops the burner and pan can be used. These shields roll up to occupy very little room in your rucksack. The whole process can be further improved by attaching a Mountain Safety Research (MSR) 'Heat Exchanger' to the pot.

10

> *Every year I hear of fatalities – simply because people do not take altitude-related symptoms seriously. They are easy to recognise and simple to treat.*
>
> *Dr Charles Clarke*

Dealing With Altitude

Altitude illness is thought to be a spectrum of problems caused by the lower availability of oxygen in the air we breathe at altitude. It is usually brought on by rapid travel to elevations greater than 2500 metres. Opinions vary amongst medical experts and experienced high altitude mountaineers as to the prevention and treatment of altitude illness; trekkers and mountaineers can expect to encounter conflicting advice in other publications.

ACUTE MOUNTAIN SICKNESS (AMS)

It is imperative that everyone who plans to travel, trek or climb at altitudes above 2500m has an understanding of the prevention, recognition and treatment of AMS. Specific advice for people travelling above 5000m can be found later in this chapter.

AMS usually develops during the first 36 hours at altitude, rather than immediately upon arrival. More than 50% of travellers develop some form of AMS on ascent to 3500m, but almost all do so if they ascend rapidly to 5000m. Rarely, AMS will progress to High Altitude Cerebral Oedema

(HACO/HACE) or High Altitude Pulmonary Oedema (HAPO/HACE), both of which are very serious complications of AMS.

AMS is mimicked by many other medical problems. For example, a case report in recent medical literature describes a man who was initially thought to be suffering from AMS, but who was in fact having a heart attack. Nevertheless, unless it can be medically proven that the signs and symptoms of AMS are definitely caused by another condition, then the victim must be assumed to be suffering from AMS.

Symptoms Of AMS

Symptoms of AMS include:

- Headache
- Fatigue
- Dizziness
- Poor appetite
- Nausea
- Vomiting
- Insomnia
- Irregular breathing during sleep
- A sensation of the heart beating forcibly

Prevention Of AMS

Whilst most people will have to grin and bear a few sleepless nights and a couple of pounding headaches, almost all other forms of AMS are entirely avoidable, thanks to a process known as 'acclimatisation'. It is medically proven that providing enough time is allowed, the majority of people are able to adapt to altitudes of 5000m or thereabouts. AMS can usually be prevented by resting for one or more days upon initial arrival at altitude.

Aids To Acclimatisation

There are many things you can do to increase your chance of acclimatising. Firstly, drink an adequate supply of liquid. Pale or clear urine is the only certain indication that you are drinking enough water. Bear in mind that by the time you feel thirsty, you are already dehydrated. Aim to drink several litres of water a day at altitudes above 3000m. Such a large intake of water is necessary to offset the fluid lost whilst sweating and breathing. In addition, the lack of oxygen at altitude normally triggers an increase in urinary output. Ironically, discovering that you are suddenly peeing much more than usual is a sign that the body is acclimatising. (A pee bottle - and a funnel for ladies - might prove to be a useful night-time companion). If you

are easily bored by water, it can be flavoured with fruit crystals.

Taking the time to acclimatise properly will maximise the chance of a successful summit attempt

Avoid the temptation to push yourself at altitude. A gentle and regular pace is preferable to a forced march. However, it should be noted that gaining altitude slowly can prove somewhat boring for some young people and certain adults, some of whom may feel a need to prove themselves in front of their peers. No-one has anything to prove at altitude, and it is worth noting that fit people might be more likely to contract AMS than unfit people by virtue of their ability to gain more height in a day.

Try to resist the temptation to drink alcohol during the acclimatisation phase of your trip. Do everything you can to avoid falling ill. Protect yourself against the sun, and drink and eat as much as you feel able to. A normal or increased appetite at altitude is usually an encouraging sign of acclimatisation.

The Use Of Acetazolamide (Diamox)

The drug Acetazolamide (Diamox) can be useful in the prevention of AMS. Acetazolamide is a diuretic; that is, it encourages the body to get rid of excess fluid by increasing urinary output. Acetazolamide also makes the blood more acidic, thereby encouraging the body to regulate its breathing. This is especially useful at night.

The use of Acetazolamide is controversial: many doctors and experienced mountaineers believe that under normal circumstances, drugs such as Acetazolamide should not be taken to aid ascent. As a result, many climbers and trekkers prefer to do without it. Indeed, some mountaineers argue that from an ethical point-of-view, taking any drug as an aid to ascent is a form of cheating. The UIAA Mountain Medicine Centre does not recommend using Acetazolamide as a routine drug before or during an ascent.

Acetazolamide can have side-effects, including a tingling in the extremities. Acetazolamide causes many people to feel 'off colour'. In addition, fizzy drinks may taste flat and food can taste metallic. Dizziness, vomiting, drowsiness, confusion and rashes have all been reported but these are unusual. People who are allergic to sulphonamide antibiotics may also be allergic to Acetazolamide. Exceptionally, the drug can cause more serious problems. These include disorders of blood formation, convulsions and kidney stones.

Whilst medical opinion differs over the most effective daily regime of Acetazolamide, there are many reports of climbers and trekkers who have benefited from a daily dose of 500mg. For people who decide to take Acetazolamide, the UIAA Mountain Medicine Centre suggests that 250mg is taken twice daily for two days at sea level as a trial, several weeks before a

A CAUTIONARY TALE

'The headache was the worst I had ever experienced. I found that I could find some relief by sitting propped up. Walking was impossible - I fell over. Why? Quite simply I had swelling of the brain, known as high altitude cerebral oedema (HACE) because I had travelled too quickly to about 4600m. We had driven up to the Tibetan plateau from Nepal and as ever, we were in a hurry; most of the team were well and I was holding them up. God I felt ill.

I should have lost height immediately, waited a few days and then continued up. Instead I treated myself with Dexamethasone, the potent steroid we use for HACE and the next day struggled over a 5000m pass. We were then able to drop below 4000m. Miraculously, my problems disappeared.

This is an example of what *not* to do with altitude sickness. Read the BMC website before you go to altitude!'

Dr Charles Clarke

visit to altitude. Assuming that no unpleasant side-effects are experienced, the drug may be taken in the same dose for three days before arrival at 3500m and thereafter for two or three days until one feels acclimatised.

Some doctors advise the use of Acetazolamide as a prophylactic treatment during ascent for individuals who have shown a repeated inability to acclimatise to altitudes up to 5000m. The drug may also be taken by unacclimatised rescue parties that need to ascend rapidly in order to bring down an injured person.

Treatment Of AMS

Symptoms of AMS are often concealed by people, yet it is vital that people travelling to altitude tell others around them about any possible symptoms of AMS they are experiencing. Early recognition allows prompt treatment to take place, and reduces the chances of your trip having to be cut short. People on a commercial trek or climb should not feel any 'peer pressure' to keep up with the group. Treatments for the following conditions are suggested:

Headache

Paracetamol may be taken at the rate of 1000mg every six hours. If no improvement is noticed after one dose of Paracetemol (combined with adequate re-hydration and two hours of rest) the presence of AMS should be suspected. Descent is strongly recommended. People who are unable to descend for practical reasons (e.g. snowstorm) may take Acetazolamide, which is considered to be an effective treatment of moderate symptoms of AMS. The usual dose is 250mg every 8 hours for two days.

Nausea, Dizziness And Vomiting

An antiemetic such as Prochlorperazine (Buccastem or Stemetil) for nausea, dizziness and vomiting. Note that Stemetil needs to be swallowed and so consequently it is less effective in the vomiting patient. By contrast, Buccastem simply dissolves under the tongue.

Pressure Chambers

Temporary relief from altitude illness can also be achieved with the use of a portable pressure chamber, which works by creating a lower altitude than the surroundings. Unlike bottled oxygen, chambers cannot run out of air and can be re-used. The pressure to simulate descent is obtained by means of a foot pump. Pressure chambers are particularly useful in environments such as the Tibetan Plateau, which is at a high altitude and offers little chance of a quick descent. They are also useful at night, in bad weather and

> I have found that the height of the top camp is crucial. You can deteriorate much more at a higher camp. Also, it is better to have a comfy and safe campsite than a precarious one a few hundred metres higher.

Jon Tinker

Heavy loads are best avoided until after you have acclimatised

to stabilise a severely ill person before evacuation. They may also buy sufficient time for administered drugs to take effect. The use of a chamber may be alternated with bottled oxygen.

Treatment times vary, but one or more hours may be sufficient to allow an individual with AMS, HAPE or HACE to make a supervised descent under his own steam, rather than being carried. This can make a big difference to a person's chance of survival, especially during a climbing expedition where the terrain may make carrying a person difficult.

With a victim of altitude illness – especially HAPE and HACE – the head end of the chamber should be raised by 30 degrees. This is because the fluid that collects round the lungs or brain tends to drain away more easily in the tilted position.

The use of the chamber alone is no guarantee of a complete and permanent recovery as the benefits of treatment may be lost in just a few hours. This so-called 'rebound' phenomenon may also occur during the slightest exertion. Someone who has been suffering from altitude illness should commence a supervised descent immediately upon leaving the bag.

Descent

If these treatments are ineffective or if symptoms worsen, the patient *must descend under the supervision of a healthy person.* Acetazolamide may be taken during descent. To delay supervised descent for any reason (including awaiting medical advice, or because of darkness) is to increase dramatically the chance of the victim dying. A rapid loss of height will never make any altitude-related condition worse. Normally a drop of 500-1000m is sufficient to promote spontaneous recovery. After a night or two of rest at the lower altitude, the patient may return to altitude. If the symptoms re-appear, descend again.

If a person shows signs of severe AMS then an immediate, supervised descent must be carried out. A person with severe AMS should ideally be evacuated to a hospital, and preferably one that is located no more than 1500m above sea level. The victim must not be allowed to re-ascend until he has been seen by an experienced doctor. Oxygen may be given to the patient through a face mask during the descent, at the rate of four to six litres per minute. If your group does not have oxygen, you might want to ask any other groups in the area if they have any. Do not delay supervised descent in order to obtain oxygen. Supervised descent often requires a large degree of organisation, especially if a rescue has also been requested. If the victim of severe AMS is not a stretcher case on setting out, he might become one, so plan accordingly. *You can read more about organising an evacuation in Chapter 14.*

If you decide to travel to high altitude with a commercial operator, it is a good idea to ask what relevant knowledge and experience your leader has. At the very least, he should be able to recognise and treat the signs of altitude sickness in a victim. You might also want to ask whether bottled oxygen or a pressure chamber will be carried on your trip. In addition, you could enquire about what contingencies are in place for a member of the group who needs to spend an additional day at a lower altitude in order to acclimatise.

TESTING FOR AMS (AND HACE)

There is no foolproof test for AMS and HACE. However, the following procedures can easily be carried out by someone with no medical training. The suspected victim should be tested alongside a healthy person so that a comparison may be made. A person with deteriorating AMS will invariably perform these tests so poorly (if he is able to perform them at all) that there will be no doubt in anyone's mind that a supervised descent should be undertaken immediately. Even if all three tests are carried out successfully, the presence of altitude illness cannot be ruled out. It is vital to show respect for the patient (who must be sober) whilst carrying out these assessments. Conduct the tests away from other people. If the victim fails any of the tests, reassure him that he will be all right. Begin a supervised descent immediately.

The Finger-To-Nose Test

This test has the advantage of being able to be carried out by a bed-ridden person who is sitting upright. (The fact that a person is unable get out of bed may in itself be a cause for concern.) Of the three tests, the finger-to-nose is the easiest to cheat on. Ask the patient to extend his arm out in front of his face, and then to place his index finger on his nose. The eyes should be open during this test. A healthy person will be able to touch the tip, or at the very least the edge, of his nose. Someone with AMS may end up touching his cheek, or miss his head altogether.

The Heel-To-Toe Test

Place a marker on level ground, 10 metres away from the standing patient. Ask the patient to walk heel-to-toe to the marker. The eyes must be kept open. The healthy individual will have no difficulty in completing the task, apart from the odd 'wobble'. The person with AMS may stagger, or even fall to the floor, so ensure you have someone close by to catch them if they collapse.

The Standing Test

Ask the patient to stand up straight with feet together and arms at the sides of the body, as if 'at attention'. Place your hands six inches away from each side of their body, so that you can catch them if they fall. Now ask the patient to shut his eyes (check that they have) and to try to remain standing upright. If you are unsure that the person has completely closed his eyes, blindfold him and make sure he cannot peek out of the bottom of the mask. The healthy person will remain motionless, or sway ever-so-slightly. The person suffering from AMS will sway violently, and possibly topple over. Before carrying out this test, it may be necessary to reassure the patient that you will catch them if they fall. Demonstrate the test using a healthy individual if necessary. (This test is also known as the Romberg Test.)

HIGH ALTITUDE PULMONARY OEDEMA (HAPE)

HAPE is a rare complication of AMS. It is a life-threatening condition in which fluid collects in the lungs. It will result in death by suffocation if left untreated. HAPE usually occurs at altitudes above 2500m, especially in individuals who rush to altitude or engage in a high level of physical activity. A person who is short of breath at rest, or who is unable to catch his breath after 15 minutes of complete rest, may be suffering from HAPE. A person who is coughing up bubbly, wet, pink sputum, or who can be heard to have a gurgling or clicking in the lungs (sometimes detectable in even mild cases by placing an ear to the chest) must be assumed to have HAPE.

The most effective treatment is immediate, supervised descent. Oxygen may be administered via a face mask during descent. The rate of flow will depend on the amount of oxygen available. A rate of four to six litres per minute should prove to be of benefit to the patient. The victim must not be allowed to re-ascend until he has been seen by an experienced doctor.

Nifedipine (Adalat) tablets may have a role – and have been used – in the treatment of HAPE. The UIAA Mountain Medicine Centre recommends that 20mg of oral Nifedipine is taken immediately, followed by 20mg every six hours for a period of one day. *Pressure chambers may be used in the treatment of HAPE. For details, see earlier in this chapter.*

HIGH ALTITUDE CEREBRAL OEDEMA (HACE)

HACE is another rare complication of AMS. It is swelling of the brain due to fluid accumulation and tends to occur at altitudes above 3500m. A person with HACE will show a lack of co-ordination (known as 'ataxia'). He will also have a blinding and seemingly permanent headache. Untreated cases of HACE lead to unconsciousness, coma and death.

The most effective treatment is immediate, supervised descent. The victim must not be allowed to re-ascend until he has been seen by an experienced doctor. The potent steroid Dexamethasone (Decadron) may be used in the treatment of HACE in order to buy time during descent. The UIAA Mountain Medicine Centre recommends 8mg of Dexamethasone initially, followed by 4mg every six hours for one day.

There is evidence to suggest that Dexamethasone may be effective in some people who are suffering from an incapacitating headache and who are unable to descend for practical reasons (e.g. snowstorm). In this type of situation a dose regime of 4mg initially, followed by 4mg every six hours for one day may be taken. It is worth bearing in mind that Dexamethasone can mask the onset of HACE, and that someone complaining of a severe headache might already be suffering from the condition. *Pressure chambers may be used in the treatment of HACE. For details, see earlier in this chapter.*

> ❝The average acclimatiser can climb safely to 6000 metres within two weeks of leaving sea level. But it needs to be done in incremental steps: first a slow trek to 5000 metres, then a climb to 5300 metres, then a climb to 5700 metres, with rests in between. Once you go much above 6000 metres everything becomes a bit harder and needs longer acclimatisation. However, if you take things slowly, it is perfectly possible to feel fine – and actually enjoy yourself – to above 7000 metres.❞
>
> *Stephen Venables*

TRAVELLING ABOVE 5000M

Trekkers and mountaineers will have a better time of it if they have taken the appropriate number of days to acclimatise to 5000m. Beyond this height true acclimatisation is not possible; however a slow rate of ascent may permit the body to adjust to the increasingly rarefied atmosphere. There are no firm rules for ascent when it comes to altitudes above 5000m, although previous experience normally allows the individual to fine-tune his personal acclimatisation programme on future ascents.

Life-threatening forms of altitude illness including High Altitude Pulmonary Oedema (HAPE) and High Altitude Cerebral Oedema (HACE) may occur suddenly in even well-acclimatised individuals. A debilitating cough is a common ailment. Other conditions such as a blood clot in the leg (deep vein thrombosis), blood clot in the chest (pulmonary embolus) and a weakness of one arm or leg (stroke) are brought on as a result of changes in blood clotting. These conditions are more commonly seen in individuals climbing beyond 7000m (advice on which is beyond the scope of this book).

An unfortunate side-effect of high altitude is that the reduction in available oxygen can impair many things, from blood circulation in the extremities to being able to think clearly. Of course, rational thought is vital if sound mountaineering decisions are to be made and nowhere is this more crucial than at high altitude where even a small mistake can rapidly deteriorate into a serious situation. Agreeing on summit day turnaround times before venturing above 5000m is one way to help to ensure that individuals do not push on when there is little chance of being able to make a safe return before nightfall. Having the necessary technical experience to cope with the difficulties of your intended route removes some of the pressure, allowing you to concentrate on handling the negative effects of altitude.

OTHER ISSUES AT HIGH ALTITUDE

Retinal haemorrhages

Minute blood blisters in the back of the eye (known as retinal haemorrhages) are common at around 5000m but it is rare for them to cause problems. These haemorrhages are only visible to the trained observer and interfere with eyesight very occasionally. If a person claims that he is suffering from a 'hole' in his vision, the UIAA Mountain Medicine Centre recommends descent.

Peripheral Oedema

Fluid retention in the face and limbs is known as Peripheral Oedema. It usually subsides over a period of several days and does not herald the onset of HACE or HAPE.

Oral Contraceptives

Opinion varies on whether it is safe to take oral contraceptives at altitude. The UIAA Mountain Medicine Centre reports that there is no good evidence to support anecdotal suggestions that AMS is worse in women who take oral contraceptives. There is cumulative evidence of a large number of women who have taken oral contraceptives on trekking and climbing holidays up to 5000m. No particular side-effects have been regularly noted. However, vomiting as a result of AMS might reduce the effectiveness of the oral contraceptive. *Chapter 5 contains advice on other issues surrounding the contraceptive pill.*

High Altitude Cough

Unless you have a cough that resembles the type described for HAPE, then a cough in itself is no indicator of AMS. Nevertheless, a cough can become debilitating and exhausting. Once again, prevention is far easier than cure: try to look after your throat. An attempt at regulating your breathing might help; some climbers breathe through a thin fabric facemask or scarf in cold air and at night so that the air can be slightly warmed before it hits the throat and lungs. It's worth carrying plenty of cough tablets, especially the ones that contain a local anaesthetic. Take these prophylactically if necessary. If you do develop a dry, hacking cough, try and relax when experiencing a coughing fit; severe coughing has been known to crack ribs.

Special Cases

Pregnant women, the elderly, people with existing medical conditions and adults who want to take babies and children to altitude are all strongly recommended to seek expert medical advice before travelling.

CALCULATING YOUR ACCLIMATISATION PROGRAMME

The minimum acclimatisation period for any altitude greater than 2500m is to sleep no more than 300m higher than your previous night's camp, and to spend an extra night at every third camp. An individual being taken passively to altitudes above 2500m (such as Cusco in Peru and Leh in India) should spend the appropriate number of additional nights at the altitude they have arrived at, in order to allow the body to 'catch up'.

However, finding somewhere to stay at every 300m mark can prove difficult, as the following example illustrates:

Typical acclimatisation programme for individuals trekking from Lukla to Gorak Shep, in the Khumbu (Everest) region of Nepal.

Day 1:   Fly Lukla (2850m). Trek to and overnight at Phakding (2621m)
Day 2:   Trek to Namche Bazaar (3446m)
Day 3:   Rest day in Namche
Day 4:   Rest day in Namche
Day 5:   Trek to Tengboche (3867)
Day 6:   Rest day Tengboche
Day 7:   Trek to Periche (4252m)
Day 8:   Rest day Periche
Day 9:   Trek to Dughla (4620m)
Day 10: Trek to Loboje (4930m)
Day 11: Rest day in Loboje
Day 12: Trek to Gorak Shep (5184m)

Notes For This Chapter

1. Self diagnosis is to be heavily discouraged, even when the patient is a qualified doctor. This applies to every medical condition. Precise clinical diagnosis without modern laboratory facilities can be very difficult, even for highly skilled medical doctors. Many different diseases can mimic each other with their symptoms.

2. Anyone taking any medication should be aware of potential recorded side-effects, written details of which should be supplied with the drug by the dispensing chemist.

As you can see, the height gain from the lowest camp to the highest camp is 2563m. Divided by 300m, the ideal number of nights spent on trek would be nine, plus three additional rest days, and indeed the acclimatisation programme in the table takes 12 days. It should be noted that the jump of 825m on the second day is far from ideal; hence the mandatory rest days at Namche and Tengboche.

A two or three week trek in the Himalaya provides an ideal time frame to adjust to altitude. AMS problems are more common on mountains like Kilimanjaro (5895m) where six-day ascents are considered normal by some tour operators. During these rapid ascents to altitude, the chance of contracting a life-threatening altitude-related illness increases dramatically. There is a solution, and the solution is time. In some cases, just a couple of extra days will allow for adequate acclimatisation. This will increase your chance of enjoying a safe and successful trip. The financial cost of these additional days is small when compared to the overall expense of the adventure. If you simply have no more time, then you might want to re-consider the height that you would like to reach. If you decide to trek with an operator, you might ask to see the daily schedule and height of overnight camps on the trip you are interested in. You can then apply this acclimatisation formula to the company's timetable, in order to see if the programme is attainable.

It is quite permissible to climb higher than 300m during the day, providing that you return to the appropriate height to sleep. This is known as 'climbing high, sleeping low'. It is an effective way for the body to 'taste' a higher altitude prior to sleeping at such a height. If you are feeling strong, then it can be quite a useful exercise to adopt such a strategy on your rest days. Climbing high and sleeping low also allows you to reach a summit, or cross a high pass, without having to fully acclimatise to that altitude. In the case of the Everest trek, it would be possible to climb the small peak of Kalar Pattar (5623m) the day after arriving at Gorak Shep, providing that you returned to Gorak Shep or Loboje to sleep.

YOUR QUESTIONS ANSWERED

My friend has altitude sickness but we can't descend because we're trapped between two high passes. What should we do?

This is a difficult situation. If your friend has suspected altitude sickness and is deteriorating, then administer what altitude-related drugs you have. Ask other people (including trekkers and locals) to help you. Check your map, or ask if there is a way down to the bottom of a valley that does not require you to ascend to the top of one of the passes; a descent of just 500m may be enough to promote a complete recovery. If there is no choice but to ascend to the top of one of the passes in order to effect a subsequent descent, find out which pass offers the greatest subsequent loss of altitude. If advice or a map is not available, return the way you have come (better the devil you know) unless you know the drop on the other side is less than the height you are currently at. A prompt evacuation is important but avoid rushing: take food, water, medicines and shelter with you even if you have to abandon other supplies. If you are completely alone and have no-one else to call on for support, then you will need to think clearly. Ascending with your friend and the bare amount of survival equipment is one option. Once you have started, don't stop until you have crossed the pass and have dropped down to a safe elevation. Do not underestimate the amount of effort this will entail. You will know when you have reached the correct altitude as your friend will make a rapid recovery. If your friend is unable to walk, then you may have no option but to leave him in order to summon help.

11

> Being disabled doesn't mean that you are excluded from mountain environments, which are a sanctuary for everyone. A lack of imagination and creativity are the only barriers to their enjoyment.

Karen Darke

ADDITIONAL CONSIDERATIONS

This chapter includes supplemental information for parents and children, mature trekkers, disabled adventurers and women.

PARENTS AND CHILDREN

Trekking with children can be an enlightening and thoroughly enjoyable experience for all concerned. Nevertheless, there are a number of precautions that parents and guardians are advised to take before and during mountain journeys with their children. These include:

Prior Experience

Give a lot of thought to the trek you would like to attempt with your family. If the adults in the party have never visited the country before, is it wise to head there with young children? Choosing a destination where the majority of the population understands a language in which you are fluent could prove to be of immense benefit if a tricky situation arises.

Children may try to run down steep paths, stroke domestic animals and bounce up and down on rickety bridges so parents will need to be

constantly vigilant. Think about your own ambitions whilst on holiday with your family. One parent is known to have made the ascent of a 6000m peak in the Himalaya with his one-year-old son strapped to his back; not the best example of minimising risk.

Parents and children are likely to have a better time on treks abroad if they have already become accustomed to walking and camping in the UK. There's usually no need for a rucksack brimming with toys as bazaars are full of colourful trinkets, and children are masters of improvisation.

Camping is an exciting new world for young children

Clothing And Equipment

A child needs to be dressed in appropriate attire for the temperature and conditions you expect to encounter. An increasing number of outdoor retailers stock clothing for children. Alternatively, materials such as fleece and waterproof nylon can be bought off the roll. Garments can then be produced to your specification by a friendly local seamstress or tailor. *Appendix A contains contact details for specialist retailers of outdoor clothing for children.*

There is good medical evidence that sunburn in childhood predisposes the victim to skin cancer later in life. It is important for children to wear clothes that protect them from the sun, and to apply suncream regularly to exposed skin. *Suncreams are discussed in Chapter 5.*

Rather than investing in a child's sleeping bag, why not purchase an adult bag, and simply alter the length of the bag with a belt? As your child grows, the belt can be moved down the bag.

A child who weighs less than 25kg can usually be transported in a purpose-built carrier. A variety of rucksack-style models are now available. A dedicated sun and rain shade can be attached to some designs or you can improvise with an umbrella. Be aware that many carriers will topple over if left unsupported when you place them on the ground. It is advisable to buy a model that has a built-in shoulder harness system. That way, if you stumble forward the child is less likely to fall out.

In chilly weather, check regularly that the toddler is wearing enough clothing to prevent the onset of hypothermia. Compare the temperature of the feet or hands to the torso. If the trunk is much warmer than the extremities then the child is too cool. It is a sad fact that deaths occur every year as a result of hypothermia in children who have been carried by parents who go out walking and skiing in the European Alps.

A tent will provide your child with a relaxing and familiar environment at the end of each day, especially if you have already practised a few overnight stays under canvas prior to departure. A tent also provides a welcome respite from the new world they are exploring – being stared at by curious onlookers can be exhausting!

Safety Equipment

It makes sense to bring any safety equipment that is deemed necessary with you. This might include a correctly-sized climbing harness and helmet. Very young climbers are encouraged to wear a scaled-down full-body harness that has attachment points at the chest and waist rather than a sit harness, as it is possible for children to slip out of the latter design.

Toilet Habits

Single-use nappies are likely to prove difficult to dispose of. Diapers soaked in kerosene burn poorly, whilst many religions treat fires as sacred. Reusable nappies are ideal, but take care to wash them out of sight of others in order to avoid offending local people. A collapsible bucket will allow you to clean the diapers away from water sources such as streams. Most children under the age of five prefer a potty to the somewhat intimidating squat-loo found in many mountain villages.

Medical Considerations

The time and distance to a centre of medical excellence should be borne in mind when choosing a place to trek, although day-to-day problems like diarrhoea are likely to prove the most troublesome. Young children experiment by putting things in their mouths, which further increases the likelihood of faecal-oral contamination. Dehydration in a child – brought on by diarrhoea or vomiting – can be life-threatening: parents must know about oral rehydration in order to deal with this condition. Other conditions, such as malaria, are also dangerous. A malaria-free destination is by far the best bet when travelling with small children.

CHILDREN AND ALTITUDE

If your children are too young to describe how they are feeling then altitude illness is likely to prove difficult to diagnose. In this situation it is a good idea to limit the maximum altitude on a trek to 3000m. Any gain in height should be achieved very gradually, and parents are recommended to avoid taking children to altitude by air or road: walking up from a low altitude is much the preferred option. Avoid taking children who are suffering from colds or coughs to altitude as some doctors believe that these conditions increase the risk of altitude illness.

Parents and guardians who plan to take children into the mountain environment are strongly urged to seek the opinion of a medical doctor with appropriate experience before departure, especially if the child has a pre-existing medical condition. *Appendix A includes details of medical organisations, whilst Appendix E includes details of books dedicated to travelling with children.*

❝ If you have got a fortnight's trekking holiday, don't ruin it by trying to walk six or seven hours from day one. Build up to it. It's much better than having to grit your teeth for the entire holiday against the pain of strains and injuries sustained in the first day or two. ❞

Tim Salmon

THE MATURE TREKKER

Walking in the mountains can be an ideal activity for the mature person who has not trekked before as there is no particular skill to learn in order to undertake the activity. One can make the experience as demanding or relaxing as one likes, from half-day treks beginning from the comfort of a well-equipped mountain lodge, to multi-day camping expeditions. The popular trails in many countries are graded for their level of difficulty, which makes it reasonably straightforward to find a route to suit your fitness and ambitions. It is worth remembering that if you are left feeling exhausted at the end of a day, a single night's sleep under canvas may not be sufficient to leave you feeling refreshed the next morning: look carefully at the proposed itinerary to make sure it is all within your capabilities.

Depending on your existing level of conditioning and the nature of the undertaking, you might need to exercise several times a week during the months leading up to departure. Many treks by their very nature involve a fair amount of ascent and descent: prospective trekkers will want to ensure that they can tackle the expected gradients by undertaking similar ascents in the UK hills.

If the idea of trekking appeals, but the thought of plodding up and down potentially steep slopes does not, then you merely need to seek out walks that follow valley floors, or explore the relatively flat plains that surround certain mountain ranges such as the Patagonian Andes and Pamir mountains of Central Asia. A handful of tour operators organise treks for people over a certain age. The pace of these journeys is invariably more gentle than on regular trips. The groups are usually friendly and relaxed, and devoid of any of the competitive pressure that sometimes builds up in parties that include younger people. The chance of being struck down with altitude illness is the same for older people as it is for younger trekkers. However, the fact that an older person is likely to gain height at a slow rate bodes well for avoiding medical conditions such as Acute Mountain Sickness. *You can read more about altitude illness in Chapter 10.*

When it comes to climbing there are plenty of septuagenarian mountaineers, and an increasing number of people in their 50s and 60s are making ascents of the Himalayan giants, including Everest. However, it would be fair to say that most of the people who achieve these feats are highly experienced and fit mountaineers who have been climbing for many years. If you have any doubts about your fitness, explain to your doctor what you are proposing to undertake, and ask for a health check up before commencing any form of physical exercise. A comprehensive travel insurance policy that covers your age group is highly recommended. *You can read more about insurance policies in Chapter 5.*

DISABLED ADVENTURERS

Disabled people heading for the mountain environment will probably find that they need to spend extra time planning their climb or trek. With the correct level of fitness and preparation, almost every type of mountain activity can be enjoyed. In recent years a wheelchair adventurer has travelled through the foothills of the Himalaya and both a blind mountaineer and an amputee have reached the summit of Everest. Every individual will want to adapt the broad suggestions outlined here to suit his own particular condition.

Logistics

In addition to the hurdles of transportation, the mountaineer or backpacker operating beyond the reach of towns and villages will need to ensure that he has sufficient spare parts for any essential equipment (such as hearing aid batteries or a wheelchair puncture repair kit). Bear in mind that extra gear might require additional porters or pack animals to transport it.

> Integrated expeditions consisting of able-bodied and disabled people can work providing that everyone is involved in the planning from the outset.
>
> *Glenn Shaw*

Medical

The level of specialist day-to-day and emergency medical care the mountain traveller requires will determine the level of support needed. Options range from being accompanied by a medically-trained person (who has the relevant mountain experience) to a satellite telephone link to a doctor. *Chapter 14 contains information on satellite telephones and other forms of remote communication.*

It is recommended that at least double the normal quantity of essential medication is divided amongst two or more people in case one supply is lost or spoiled.

Integration

Whilst some experienced disabled climbers and trekkers organise their own expeditions and even undertake solo journeys into the mountains, the inexperienced mountain adventurer will probably want to join a group. If you sign up with an organisation, you might be the only disabled person in the team, or one of several.

An expedition organiser who wishes to invite a disabled person to join the team would do well to give a lot of thought to the role that the individual will perform in the field. Why not talk through the various options with the candidate? For example, a wheelchair user might be the Base Camp Manager on a mountaineering expedition, whilst a blind trekker could be the ideal person to handle satellite radio interviews on a charity trek. Of course, the disabled mountaineer or instructor who has an appropriate level of experience could be the leader or assistant leader in the mountain activity they specialise in.

There may be times when the disabled adventurer needs assistance. By training together, members of an integrated team will know instinctively when and when not to offer assistance to one another.

There is no reason why, with the appropriate level of training and preparation, the disabled mountaineer or trekker should not play an equal part in the planning, execution and post-trip phases of almost any project *and* fulfil a valuable role within the team.

The different perspective that each individual brings to the project is likely to enhance the experience for everyone on the trip or expedition. *Appendix A includes a number of specialist organisations that cater for disabled people.*

Women are often welcomed with open arms into local communities

WOMEN

Experienced female mountaineers have suggested the following tips for comfort whilst travelling:

- Wear a sarong while bathing to avoid drawing attention to yourself
- Use a damp sponge or pre-moistened tissues for a quick wash
- Carry a small amount of moisturiser in a tiny screw-top plastic bottle
- Smear Vaseline on the inside of thighs to prevent chaffing
- Consider carrying the appropriate treatments for cystitis and thrush

Travel, exercise and altitude often change menstrual cycles. There are also issues surrounding oral contraceptives and deep vein thrombosis (DVT). Women who require (or may require) contraception during their journey are advised to seek advice from their doctor in advance of their departure. If you do choose to take oral contraception during your trip, it's definitely worth packing a supply of condoms (either of the male or female variety) in case you suffer an attack of diarrhoea or vomiting as these conditions can reduce the effectiveness of the contraceptive pill. Some antibiotics also reduce the contraceptive pill's effectiveness. Pregnant women planning to travel abroad are strongly recommended to speak to their GP before making any travel arrangements.

All women are encouraged to take an ample supply of sanitary products from home (in a watertight container) as supplies in certain countries may be limited. Some female trekkers place their used sanitary products in re-sealable plastic bags and carry them in the side pockets of their rucksacks until an appropriate place of disposal can be found. This is an excellent policy, but be aware that in some mountain communities the waste from toilets is used as fertiliser. Whilst on the subject of lavatories, quite often there may be nowhere obvious to go to the loo. In these situations, a baggy elasticated skirt (carried for the purpose) can be quickly pulled on or an umbrella can be unfolded. *Issues surrounding taking the oral contraceptive at altitude are discussed in Chapter 10.*

Clothing

There is now a profusion of outdoor clothing and equipment on the market that has been designed specifically for women; the days of having to make do with a waterproof jacket that is too long in the arms and too narrow at the hips are long gone. If the culture of the country you are in encourages you not to draw attention to yourself in public, consider wearing loose clothing that covers the arms, legs, midriff and cleavage, as well as items that disguise the contours of the body. *You can read about other cultural aspects in Chapter 4.*

There is anecdotal evidence that a percentage of women feel the cold quite considerably. If you think that this might apply to you, consider buying a sleeping bag designed for use in colder temperatures than you expect to encounter and pack extra clothing (including hats and mitts). A leakproof water bottle can work wonders; fill it with boiling hot water and pop it in your sleeping bag an hour or so before you retire for the night. In the morning, the lukewarm liquid can be used for washing.

Some women prefer to wear a sports bra instead of a regular model, especially when driving along bumpy roads. Bras – especially underwired models – can also cause pressure sores: having more than one design in your rucksack can help to alleviate any discomfort. A trouser belt can come in handy if you find the mountain diet begins to have an effect on your figure.

Getting Things Organised

In certain male-dominated societies it might be difficult for officials and operators to accept that you are making your own travel arrangements. It is not uncommon for a woman travelling with a male companion to ask all the questions, but for all the answers to be directed at the man. Keeping a level head, a sense of humour and making it clear that you know what you are talking about will go a long way to overcoming this type of (usually unintentional) prejudice. A grasp of essential words in the language of the country you are visiting is often a great help.

Travelling To And In The Mountains

Whilst women may find that they are barred from entering certain religious sites, they will often be welcomed with open arms in places such as Buddhist nunneries. Public transport can be an excellent place to strike up conversations with other women. Being able to ask a few simple questions in the local dialect can be an effective icebreaker. Other women will almost certainly be interested to see any pictures of your family: it might be worthwhile having three or four photographs laminated for this very purpose.

The majority of trekking guidebooks recommend that independent female trekkers should avoid travelling alone in the mountains. Travelling with a local guide (who may be male or female) is highly recommended as it is not unusual for isolated mountain communities to view the arrival of a solo female backpacker with sheer disbelief or downright suspicion. A woman hiking on her own along a remote mountain path could find herself at a severe disadvantage if she were to run into trouble. A final tip: if you do trek on your own with just a male guide for company, do take the time to check his references. Better still, obtain a recent personal recommendation from another woman. *You can read more about the potential dangers of travelling alone in Chapter 6.*

‘Sunlight at altitude can be ferociously harsh so splash on that sunscreen. Other essential items include: a hat or scarf to hide away filthy hair, lip salve and lots of water. Yes, water is heavy, but at altitude it's the one thing that will keep you well.’

Rebecca Stephens

YOUR QUESTIONS ANSWERED

What is the best way to deal with unwanted attention?

Whilst a foreign woman need not always feel compelled to act and dress like a local woman, it is useful to bear in mind that societies that have had little or no direct contact with westerners, but who have been exposed to elements of western media, might have inaccurate expectations of western women. Avoiding any physical contact and dressing soberly are two ways to ensure that your body language is not misinterpreted. If a man does make an unwelcome advance, a reply that makes it clear that you think of your new friend as a brother often goes a long way to defusing such situations. If a more aggressive move is made by a man, then shouting and drawing attention to your predicament will almost always bring people in the vicinity to your aid.

> At the beginning of my expedition life I was a member on big expeditions. I used my knowledge and climbing skill to help fulfil the expedition leader's idea. But I learnt quite quickly that this was not the right climbing style for the 1970s. So I found my own style on very small and cheap expeditions. I looked for good climbing partners. And from that moment onwards I was able to finance my own expeditions. My attitude was, 'Let's see, let's go. If we fail we will learn something. Then we will go back'. Since my expeditions were very cheap I could also afford to fail.

Reinhold Messner

SPECIFIC CONSIDERATIONS FOR EXPEDITIONS

When does an independently organised mountain adventure cross the invisible line that differentiates a simple climb or trek from a fully-fledged expedition? Some might say it depends on the size of the party. However, mountaineers have climbed Mount Everest solo and most observers would agree that these ascents are true expeditions. Others decree that a holiday only becomes an expedition if a written report is produced at the end of the project. A report allows the wider mountaineering community to learn about the team's discoveries and achievements, and can help future expeditions to plan their own ascents and explorations. Yet there are many mountain travellers who go about their business without telling a soul, yet carry out as much planning as teams that announce their intentions.

Many expeditions involve a degree of uncertainty as to their outcome and so require an element of research. Inevitably perhaps, a degree of formality will set in during this planning phase. At the end of the day, one person's holiday is another person's expedition, but every project will almost certainly be a learning process for all concerned.

The suggestions outlined here supplement the subjects discussed in the rest of the book and are aimed at the first-time expedition organiser who already knows his objective; after your first venture you will no doubt have found your own way of doing things and so will need no further advice in this regard. But a few pointers can be helpful when you are dipping your toes into expeditionary waters for the first time. There are also a handful of notes here for the expeditioner – inexperienced or otherwise – who is thinking of trying his hand at the sponsorship and publicity game. *Chapter 1 contains advice for people searching for a suitable mountain objective.*

CHOOSING A TEAM

The members of your team could be mountaineering or trekking friends. However, some projects require individuals to have additional areas of expertise that your existing circle of travelling partners do not possess. For example, you might need someone who speaks the language of the country you are visiting. People with relevant skills might be found by widening your network of contacts and those of the other members of the team. Or you could make a formal approach to an organisation like the Expedition Advisory Centre, which holds the contact details of people who are looking to join a venture on their register of personnel available for expeditions. *Appendix A includes contact details for the Expedition Advisory Centre.*

Some expedition leaders prefer a more regimented selection procedure. If you choose to go down this road, try to make any selection course resemble the proposed expedition as closely as possible. This will help you in the decision-making process, and let the participants know what they are letting themselves in for.

Regardless of whether all the team members know each other, it is nearly always necessary to organise one or more trips into your local hills before departure in order to test equipment and to discover if all the members get on with each other. If there is a clash of personalities, then hard questions might need to be asked with regard to whether everyone should go on the expedition. These questions are best answered before departure.

Even if all the team members appear to get on well with each other, it is worth bearing in mind that all the individuals will have their own slightly different ideas about fulfilling the objectives and how the team will work together. In order to create a united sense of purpose, plans need to be discussed on a regular basis.

It is worth giving some thought to the appropriate size of the party. There can be a temptation to take along a lot of people if the trekking or climbing permits are a fixed cost, or if a certain number of members guarantees a reduction in the air fare. On the other hand, more people means more food and equipment, which can result in logistical problems. A so-called 'lightweight' expedition with a small number of members and only a few local staff (or none at all) can be much easier to manage than an unwieldy team and an entourage of assistants.

A small team in a high place

The unsung hero of many expeditions is the contact person back at home. Ideally, this individual will have some prior expedition experience, and thus be able to deal with relaying any bad news, handling sponsors and the media, and reassuring any anxious relatives or close friends of members of the expedition.

In the event of an incident, the expedition will attempt to speak to the home contact who will have in his possession a duplicate set of information including the next-of-kin (NOK) details for every member of the team, the names and telephone numbers of embassy officials, and a copy of the expedition's insurance policy. In this way, the home contact can become a valuable resource in the event of a situation developing that the expedition is unable to deal with.

> "Only choose team-mates with a sense of humour."
>
> *Caroline Hamilton*

CARRYING OUT A RISK ASSESSMENT

Experienced mountaineers and backpackers are forever thinking about
every potential difficulty they might be faced with. Questions like 'Is this
route exposed to rockfall?', continually spin around inside their heads. The
term 'risk assessment' has been coined to describe the formal process of
weighing up all the foreseeable hazards and putting them down on paper.
By doing this an expedition might be able to avoid many dangers.
Furthermore, there will be a written plan of action to take in the event that
an anticipated difficulty arises. Whilst it is possible for a situation to develop
that no-one could foresee, a well thought-through risk assessment will
lessen the chance of this happening. The most useful risk assessments are
drawn up by the whole team and regularly re-assessed and up-dated
throughout the life of the expedition.

Much of the information required to complete your risk assessment will
become available before departure, but inevitably it will not be possible to
evaluate certain potential hazards (such as the depth of a river that needs to
be forded) until you are faced with the actual difficulty. Data on other
potential hazards (e.g. the weather) will need to be continually updated
during the expedition. A thorough risk assessment takes into account all the
potential difficulties that might occur.

There is an almost limitless number of questions the members of an expedition might ask themselves regarding the potential hazards on their trek or climb. Some of the more common hazards include:

- Altitude
- Rockfall and avalanche
- Animals
- River crossings
- Driving accidents (especially at night)
- Contaminated water and food

Of course, every expedition is unique and will – to one degree or other – face unique challenges regardless of how well-trodden the chosen route is. By asking potentially awkward questions early on in the project, the team will find itself with ample time to find a solution or adjust its objectives to minimise a particular hazard.

When a potential hazard has been identified, the following questions need to be asked of it:

- How likely is it that the potential hazard will become a real one?
- Is everyone at equal risk?
- What steps can be taken to minimise the risk?
- What might happen if the hazard manifests itself?
- What contingencies are in place to deal with the consequences?

A well thought-out risk assessment is often tied to the medical support for the expedition.

> ‘On expeditions, a leader is usually involved with fulfilling the dreams of several people so expect different – even hostile – reactions to any changes of plan. Don't bluff, but don't be swayed from what you know is right by the weight of contrary opinion.’
>
> *Henry Todd*

MEDICAL CONSIDERATIONS

To work out what type of medical support the expedition needs, the team might want to answer a number of questions, including:

- How long will the expedition be away for?
- How harsh is the physical environment and what are the hazards?
- What is the maximum distance (or height) a member might find himself away from base camp?
- How many people are going (including all local staff)?
- What is the available budget for medical support?
- How far away is the expedition from the nearest centre of medical excellence?

The answers to these questions will allow the member of the team appointed to handle medical matters to obtain the appropriate supplies and investigate which insurance policies cover the expedition's planned activities. *You can read about insurance in Chapter 5.*

Some teams have been known to cross-match the blood groups of the individual members. In an emergency, blood can then be taken from one or more of the team and be given to the victim. This can be particularly useful in developing countries where blood screening may not be as rigorous as one would like.

Mountaineers operating from a fixed base camp often find that a pyramid deployment of medical supplies works quite well. The majority of medical supplies can be left at the foot of the mountain. Each climbing partnership then carries between them a much smaller kit which includes remedies for the most likely illnesses and injuries. *Appendix D contains the contents for a suggested medical kit.*

Walkie-talkies can sometimes play a vital role in summoning assistance from other team members in the event of a serious incident, whilst long-range radios and satellite telephones may be used to summon outside support. However, electronic equipment is easily broken and so expeditions are cautioned against developing an over-reliance on radios and telephones if they decide to take such equipment with them. *Different methods of communication are discussed in Chapter 14.*

BUREAUCRACY

Depending on the country in which your expedition is taking place, you might find yourself filling out dozens of forms in septuplicate, or have no official paperwork to deal with at all. Where permits are required, you will probably find that politeness, patience and persistence – even when things appear to be working against you – are vital if you are to succeed in securing the necessary paperwork to allow your expedition to take place. For this reason, it is worth making contact with the relevant embassy and national mountaineering association as early as possible.

Remember that if you are planning to visit a seldom-explored area, it might take weeks, months or even years to secure the necessary permissions. It is handy to have multiple copies of members' passport details in order that police checkpoints can be cleared with the minimum amount of fuss.

Many leaders have found that the commercial services of a reputable in-country operator or agent often prove invaluable during the planning of an expedition. An experienced agent is likely to have the ear of the correct official, thus ensuring that the necessary permissions are obtained. This might cost more than if you try to do it all yourself, but in certain countries the chance of the expedition getting off the ground without using a well-connected agent is virtually nil. One way to find an appropriate agent is to look through previous expedition reports, which normally mention if they made use of any such person or organisation. Some UK-based commercial expedition companies also offer this service.

DRAWING UP THE EXPEDITION TIMETABLE

Most expeditions need time. Time to choose members, to raise money, to gain the necessary permissions, to collect equipment and so on. To rationalise all of this, you might find it worthwhile to draw up an expedition timetable that lays down what needs to be achieved, by whom and by when. *Appendix B includes a list of tasks that usually need to be completed before, during and after a mountain expedition.*

LOGISTICS

As has been said earlier in this chapter, the number of people on the team will usually determine the complexity of the expedition's logistics. A two-person team heading for Alaska might need to do no more than pack

> An expedition is no place to find out that a team member gets on your nerves. Before heading off together, get to know your team mates well.
>
> *Tim Macartney-Snape*

their rucksacks, purchase a couple of airline tickets and go. A 10-strong expedition to a previously unexplored corner of the Tien Shan is likely to have to secure excess baggage allowance, obtain permissions for satellite communications, freight gas canisters in advance and order specialist equipment from manufacturers several months before departure. Small is sometimes very beautiful indeed.

OBTAINING MORE INFORMATION ABOUT YOUR CHOSEN OBJECTIVE

The more people you speak to about your plans, the more likely you are to find individuals and expedition leaders who have been to the same (or a similar) destination and who may be willing to give you the benefit of their experience. However, it is unfair to expect these people to organise your expedition for you. In order to get any sort of positive response, it is wise to show that you have done some homework on your chosen objective. At the very least you will have read books, magazines, internet sites and previous expedition reports that include references to your objective. In the unlikely event that the BMC Information Service does not have information on the country you intend to visit, you can speak to a member of BMC staff.

You might also want to consider a reconnaissance of your intended destination, especially if it is an area about which you have been able to find out very little. A recce costs money, but might save cash in the long-term. For instance, it will allow you to meet the people who are able to organise things like transport and logistics. Furthermore, you might be able to secure elusive permits. You will be able to see at first hand what supplies are available in the shops. *Organisations that may be able to provide contact details of past expeditions are included in Appendix A, along with details of libraries that hold books, maps and reports. Details of the BMC Information Service can be found on page 15.*

> By their very nature, expeditions are focused and driven events but never forget the 'fun factor'. It has to be enjoyable to be truly memorable.

Peter Hillary

MONEY

Calculating the amount of money required to pay for the expedition – and working out who is going to pay the bills – can take up more time than any other aspect of the expedition.

Budget

Drawing up a budget is an excellent way to rationalise all your financial thoughts and concerns. It is worth bearing in mind that a budget is purely a financial representation of the objectives of the expedition. If you are unable to raise the cash, you might want to re-think your ambitions.

One way to start working out the expedition budget is to list every possible cost, from air fares to porters' tips. Then find out the likely amount for each item. This will help to minimise the likelihood of any nasty financial surprises springing up during the course of the expedition. One way of finding out approximate costs is to

Counting the cost: expedition budgets need careful management

look through the financial report of previous expeditions. Another is to speak to your in-country agent (if you are using one). Take a moment to check the date of the report in order to see how relevant their figures are to the current exchange rate. Some experienced expedition leaders double the amount of their first draft, and then refine their estimates as more financial information becomes available. Even on the final draft, it is worth carrying a cash contingency of at least 10% of the overall amount in order to be able to hose money at unforeseen difficulties that crop up.

Fundraising And Sponsorship

For all the hard work and enterprise that goes into raising money for an expedition through fundraising events and sponsorship proposals, it is quite possible that your team would be better off (and considerably less stressed) if all the members simply worked additional hours or took on part-time jobs in order to pay for their places on the expedition. There are so many expeditions looking for sponsorship and support that the chance of securing a large sum of money is not very high.

> For a first expedition, 'Keep it simple, keep it small, keep it cheap.'
>
> *David Hamilton*

Sponsors
must always
receive what
you promise
them and they
should always
get more out
of it than you
do. Make sure
that you
fulfil your
obligations.

Peter Hillary

Whilst it is true that chasing sponsorship is almost always a nerve-wracking experience, when success does come it can produce a feeling not dissimilar to that of reaching a summit. If you are determined to raise funds for the expedition (or if your expedition budget is so large that you have no choice) then the following suggestions might be of interest to you.

One of the most worthwhile things you can do is build your own network of family, friends, and friends of friends who might know of companies sympathetic to your ambitions. Mountain expeditions hold a magnetic attraction for many people. However, it is worth remembering that not all companies are interested in sponsoring expeditions. Finding out in advance if the company is sympathetic towards expeditions could save you a lot of time. It's handy to know that national companies often give their regional offices or stores a sponsorship budget to support projects involving local people. If you have a large team who live in a number of different localities, it might be possible to secure a number of small sponsors.

Secondly, you might find it more profitable to target your proposal to named individuals in a few well-researched organisations than to post hundreds of similar letters that each begin 'Dear Sir/Madam...'. Be clear about what you want from the company, be it cash, products or both. The skill here lies in offering the organisation something relevant in return for their support. For example, a post-expedition lecture to the employees of a local business might be in order, whereas a national company may want to use you in an advertising campaign.

An expedition that has secured media coverage before it approaches a sponsor often becomes very attractive, especially when one considers that it can cost thousands of pounds for a full page of advertising in a magazine, and tens of thousands of pounds for a short television advertisement. An expedition that can guarantee this sort of publicity is holding a very strong hand indeed.

Displaying a huge amount of enthusiasm for your expedition is probably your best chance of financial success. Expeditions that do receive financial or product support aren't always the most worthy or exciting but they will have been tenacious. However with sponsorship comes responsibility. Never promise what you can't deliver and always deliver what you promise. Failing to do so is likely to blacklist future expeditions from approaching that particular company - and the next expedition could of course be yours! It is a sad fact that a great many expeditions fail to send even a handful of transparencies to their sponsors.

THINKING ABOUT CLIMBING EVEREST?

'I often get letters from people who have just started climbing, asking me how they can get on an expedition to climb Mount Everest. My advice every time is to put that thought to the back of your mind and get on with pursuing the enjoyable apprenticeship of climbing. Start with cragging in the UK, do some winter climbing, then build up in the Alps to get experience of glacier travel and the bigger peaks. Follow this with small peaks in the Himalaya, and then – and only then – go for Everest. But by that time you might have decided that Everest is too crowded and on the original route is a boring old snow plod, and instead go exploring on the abundance of small unclimbed peaks you can still find dotted around the world.'

Chris Bonington

Applying For Grants

A myriad of grants for mountain expeditions, as well as individuals, are available from a variety of sources. Some awards have been established for many years. Others, especially those set up by manufacturers of outdoor clothing and equipment, have come into existence more recently.

All grant-giving organisations set strict criteria which expeditions must meet if they are to be considered. You can save yourself a lot of time and effort by applying only for those grants whose criteria you satisfy. When you receive the forms, make sure you read the questions very carefully: grant administrators never cease to be amazed by the number of forms they receive that do not include the correct information. Remember that a glossy brochure is no substitute for hard facts about your project.

It would be a mistake to think that you have to be a highly experienced mountaineer in order to be awarded a grant. Whilst you will be expected to prove that you have the necessary experience to stand a reasonable chance of safely completing your objective, some grants exist for young people to get the mountain experience they need to go on to bigger things. Other awards specifically promote the exploration of previously unvisited mountain ranges, or new lines on peaks that have already been climbed by their more straightforward routes.

Some applications are judged solely on the written information received. Others require a member of the team (normally the leader) to present the expedition's plans to a panel of experts. Being armed with maps and photographs, and thinking about your answers to some of the more obvious questions that are likely to be asked, will help you to present your plans in the best possible light. The majority of grant-giving organisations do not give their approval and support to individuals or expeditions that are linked to commercial ventures, including those that concern themselves with charity fund-raising trips.

In Britain, the principle body for distributing grants to exploratory mountaineering expeditions is the Mount Everest Foundation (MEF). The MEF also administers the grant application process for the British Mountaineering Council and Mountaineering Council of Scotland, who distribute UK Sport and Sport Scotland funds respectively. *Appendix A includes the contact details for the MEF.*

HANDLING THE MEDIA

The media can be a double-edged sword. They can promote your expedition, help you to attract sponsors and provide you with a way of repaying your supporters through 'plugs' in interviews and articles. (As a general rule of thumb, one appropriate mention of a single sponsor is usually ignored by the interviewer – more than that and expect to be cut off and not invited back.) However, if an incident befalls your team, you can expect the press to sniff around your expedition like a pack of vultures stalking a wounded animal. This might prove difficult to cope with.

If you are sure that you want to attract publicity, start with local radio and newspapers. The stories that they cover are sometimes picked up by the nationals. This tactic is likely to pay dividends right from the outset, as the most likely source of sponsorship is from local businesses. Bear in mind that the media itself is unlikely to be a source of sponsorship. They may be willing to report your progress but are unlikely to pay for interviews. It is a mutually beneficial relationship. You have something they need (a newsworthy story); they have something you want (publicity to attract a sponsor).

You might worry about whether it is best to secure sponsorship or media coverage first. Probably the best course of action is to go after both simultaneously. If a major sponsor shows an interest in you then they will almost certainly want to take over the running of any media campaign. As a general rule, for every pound a large company gives an expedition, it spends another pound advertising the fact that it has done so. That's not to say you should allow yourself to become a puppet of the sponsor. The sponsor's public relations (PR) department or agency can only put out the details that you give them, so try to make this information accurate. At the same time you will need to give the PR team appropriate stories so that they can get the media interested. Make sure that the team presents a united front, even if there are disagreements behind-the-scenes. A divided team will make a great story but for all the wrong reasons, and your sponsor will not thank you if a project they have associated themselves with becomes known for being riddled with dissent and public arguments.

If you opt to approach the media directly, try to circulate relevant stories. Local newspapers will be interested in hearing about the expedition member who lives in the same area that the paper is distributed in. By contrast, national television news programmes are likely to want to focus on what makes your adventure unique.

YOUR QUESTIONS ANSWERED

What needs to be done when the expedition returns home?

It is very easy to allow an expedition to end the moment that it arrives back home. The team will be tired - both physically and mentally - and there will be many pressing demands placed upon each of them, from spending time with family members and returning to work or college, to dealing with personal correspondence that has accumulated.

Yet the experienced expeditioner will know that the project is not quite over. Local people who assisted the team need to be written to, sponsors will expect you to honour any promises made and grant-giving organisations will invariably expect an expedition report to be submitted. This should catalogue the life of the expedition including a record of its successes and failures, as well as any and all useful information which can act as a benchmark for future expeditions planning similar projects. Even private expeditions that have received no such backing are invited to write a report and submit it to organisations such as the Alpine Club and the Expedition Advisory Centre. An inexpensively bound and typed report can (if nothing else) sit on your bookshelf as a permanent reminder of your achievements, and serve as a useful aide memoire when you begin planning your next expedition.

There are also opportunities to generate extra cash - perhaps to pay off any deficit in the budget - by giving public lectures or approaching newspapers or magazines to find out if they would be interested in a story about the trip. The aspiring writer will have approached various editors before departure in order to prepare the ground for his return.

13

> ❝Choice of gear – particularly clothing layers – is a personal thing. Don't be swayed by your climbing partner's opinions or by manufacturers' blandishments. Take what you know works and try it out before you leave. ❞
>
> *Stephen Venables*

The Contents Of Your Rucksack

If you are in possession of the clothing and equipment to walk, climb or camp in the British hills, then it is likely that you already own at least 80% of the gear that is required to undertake the same activity abroad in similar weather conditions to those you normally experience.

When it comes to buying new equipment, some people have been known to rush into their nearest outdoor store with a long list of items and feel compelled to buy only top-of-the-range gear. This approach can quickly eclipse the cost of the holiday. Other mountain travellers prefer to weigh up the pros and cons of individual items, in order to choose products within their budget that will perform satisfactorily.

CLOTHING

In an ideal world, we would each own one piece of clothing that kept the wind, rain, snow and sun out, allowed our sweat to escape, kept us warm when it was cold and cool when it was hot. A single piece of clothing that does all of this is still a pipe dream. However, it is possible to achieve all of these things with just a very few items of clothing.

It is important to remember that there are two ways to get wet; from within (perspiration) and from outside (precipitation). Perspiration can be a big problem. To prevent your clothes from being saturated by sweat, whilst at the same time remaining warm, it is necessary to wear fabrics that are able to draw perspiration away from the skin (a process commonly referred to as 'wicking') and retain body heat.

The wicking role is performed by the layer of clothing worn next-to-the-skin, which is known as the 'base layer'. The task of heat retention falls to the one or more items of clothing (collectively called the 'mid-layer') worn on top of the base layer. If you want to feel cool, wear a single base layer of clothing; if you need to stay warm, add additional mid-layer garments. Two thin layers trap more heat than one thick piece of clothing.

The most effective fabrics for wicking and retaining heat are made from synthetic fabrics, such as fleece, which do not absorb moisture. It is interesting to note that most natural materials, including cotton and silk, retain wetness within their fibres. (Wool clothing continues to work when wet but can take an age to dry.) Damp clothing is bad news because it forces the body to generate more heat, which can lead to a lowering of body temperature. Ultimately this can result in hypothermia. Even in mild conditions, a slight wind on a damp cotton shirt can rapidly chill the body. By all means take a cotton shirt or two, but undoubtedly you'll be grateful for a dry synthetic base layer to change into if the weather turns foul or when you stop and cool down.

Fending Off The Elements

When it comes to keeping rain, wind and snow out, you might think that a straightforward waterproof fabric would do the job. You'd be right, except for one thing: all the sweat vapour that has passed through the other layers of clothing that you are wearing would run up against this impenetrable barrier and condense. This is the reason why some people think their waterproof jackets leak. To combat this problem, most modern waterproof jackets are also 'breathable'; that is, they allow the sweat vapour to pass through the material. Note that breathable fabrics only allow sweat *vapour* to pass through: if the sweat vapour condenses before it reaches this waterproof/breathable outer layer then you will end up with the same condensation problem that a waterproof-only jacket would have created. In order to minimise the chance of this happening, remove mid-layers of

> Wear base layer knickers that wick sweat away and stay dry. Why? Because otherwise – having invested possibly hundreds of pounds in an expensive layering system to combat the worst weather on the planet – your cotton underwear will absorb all your sweat, resulting in damp nether regions!

Jerry Gore

clothing if you begin to feel hot, so that you are able to remain at a comfortable temperature.

Some outer layers are described as 'windproof', 'weatherproof', or 'water resistant', which means they are not guaranteed to be waterproof. (By contrast, all 'waterproof' materials are by their very nature windproof). If you are unsure if a garment is waterproof or not, turn it inside out and look at the stitching. If the manufacturer has gone to the trouble of applying tape to the seams, to prevent water from entering through the stitch holes, then it is a fair bet that the whole garment is waterproof. Of course, you will have to decide whether a 100% waterproof jacket is necessary. If rain is unlikely, then a weatherproof or similar garment (which might be cheaper and lighter than a full waterproof) might be a better option, especially if you decide to take along that unsung hero of many treks, an umbrella. A lightweight, telescopic umbrella keeps the rain off, allows you to hold conversations in foul weather, and also works as a shade when the sun appears.

Regulating Your Temperature

One easy way to regulate your temperature in cold weather is to add or remove a hat and gloves. This can make a noticeable difference to your comfort level, and is quicker than stopping to put on or take off jackets and trousers. (If you don't like wearing hoods, make sure your hat has a waterproof skin). If your clothing has underarm 'pit' zips or adjustable wrist cuffs then these can also be adjusted to quickly improve your level of comfort.

In cold weather, windproof fleece gloves are great when you want to operate a camera or open a bar of chocolate. However, a single finger produces only a small amount of heat. By contrast, a pair of mittens allows the fingers to share the warmth generated by the whole hand. A tube of material worn over each wrist helps to prevent heat escaping from the blood vessels before it reaches your fingers.

Design Features

Fixed hoods, removable hoods, articulated hoods, chest pockets, waist pockets, internal mesh pockets... the number of possible features on any one garment is virtually limitless. Rather than getting carried away with all these bells and whistles, it may be better to try the product on and see if the length and fit of the garment roughly conforms to your body shape. When you have found one or two that aren't too long, too short, too baggy or too restrictive, you can then start comparing the varying design features (especially the hood) and make an informed choice. It is worth bearing in

'Better to buy a simple coat and have enough money leftover to go away next weekend, than to buy a more expensive one and be forced to stay home because you're broke.'

John Cousins

mind that a jacket with multiple features, but made from a low-specification material, will often be a similar price to a garment that uses a higher quality fabric but sports fewer pockets and zips.

More Types Of Clothing

Some stores sell all-in-one jackets: these consist of a fleece jacket or synthetic wadding permanently attached to a waterproof material. This type of coat is best avoided, as it offers little in the way of versatility.

Another type of all-in-one garment, consisting of a fleece or fibre-pile material bonded to a highly breathable and weatherproof outer, is becoming increasingly common. This type of garment eschews the conventional layering principle; it is designed to be worn next-to-the-skin, without a base or outer layer. Cunningly placed ventilation zips allow cool air to pass over the skin in order to rapidly remove excess sweat and heat. When the wearer has achieved a comfortable temperature the zips can be sealed to prevent any further heat loss.

A down or synthetic-filled 'duvet' jacket is normally used in cold, dry environments during periods of inactivity. A duvet jacket will trap more heat than several mid layers, and works more efficiently if a single dry base layer is worn underneath.

The sun can be scorching in mountain regions; plan ahead or be prepared to improvise

A final point: some mountain regions are in politically unstable countries. Wearing military-pattern clothing may cause trouble for both yourself and other people travelling with you. Furthermore, in a rescue situation, camouflage or disruptive pattern material (DPM) can be difficult to spot.

Protection From The Sun

Be aware that the sun's rays can penetrate clothing. If you are walking in bright conditions, a balance has to be struck between keeping cool and preventing your skin from burning. Think about the colour of your clothing. Light coloured apparel keeps the body cool, whilst dark-coloured fabrics are more effective at absorbing harmful ultra violet (UV) rays, which can easily penetrate thin or open-weave materials. A sun hat with either a wide brim or a legionnaire-style flap is likely to be a valuable piece of kit. This is especially true on glaciers, where the sun's rays can turn a snow slope into an inferno. A number of manufacturers are now adding Sun Protection Factor (SPF) and Ultraviolet Protection Factor (UPF) ratings to their clothing. These ratings are similar to those used to grade suncreams. *You can read about other ways to protect yourself from the sun in Chapter 5.*

BOOTS

It is certainly worth investing an appropriate sum of money in a well-made pair of boots. If your intention is to travel through the mountains using public transport and to only engage in day-long treks, then a pair of fabric boots with a flexible sole will probably suffice. Unlike a shoe, a boot will provide some ankle support; a twisted ankle on day one of your holiday is an experience best avoided. Fabric boots that do not have a waterproof/breathable membrane are generally lighter and cooler than a leather boot. If on the other hand you are intent on tackling the terminal moraines of a Himalayan glacier, then a semi-stiffened pair of boots (either leather or membrane-backed fabric) will probably be required.

Take your time when choosing boots. Avoid visiting shops at the weekend when they are at their busiest (and when experienced members of staff are in the mountains). Does the store have a policy of allowing the boots to be returned in an unmarked condition if they have been worn around the home and found to be a poor fit? Some stores run specialist boot fitting services that include the sale of replacement insoles that can help to neutralise a variety of mild foot problems, such as pronation. It is a good idea to visit a chiropodist or a podiatrist before you buy your boots if you have a more serious foot complaint.

'Clothing for a disabled expedition member can be very hard to obtain. I'm 4ft 10in with a 50in chest! When I went to the Himalaya, the expedition members were issued with down jackets but they didn't have one to fit me. So I had to make do with three fleece jackets and a waterproof coat.'

Glenn Shaw

Socks And Gaiters

Buy the socks you intend to wear at the same time you purchase the boots. The test socks supplied by retailers are often in a tatty condition and so provide a different feel to that of a new pair. Some people prefer to wear two pairs of socks – one thick, one thin – to reduce the risk of blisters developing. Other trekkers find that modern boots are so well-lined that a single thick pair suffices. The latter tactic also cuts down on the number of socks that need to be carried. People who can't decide between the two schools of thought will be relieved to learn that there are now socks on the market that have a thin inner sock sewn into a thicker outer sock.

An unfortunate consequence of wearing cotton socks is that the material soaks up the sweat from your foot and encourages blisters to develop. Wool and synthetic blends do not suffer from this drawback. *Treatments for blisters are described in Chapter 5.*

If you are expecting to wade through streams or march through wet grass or snow, then a pair of lightweight nylon gaiters will keep your lower leg dry. Gaiters are also effective at preventing pebbles from working their way into your boot.

CLOTHING AND FOOTWEAR FOR ALTITUDES ABOVE 5000M

A number of sub-7000m mountains – such as Denali in Alaska and Vinson in Antarctica – require a level of clothing and foot protection normally associated with 8000m peaks. By contrast, certain other mountains (including Kilimanjaro in Africa) might need little more than a duvet jacket, warm mitts and a balaclava to be added to the ensemble required for trekking and climbing up to 5000m.

Mountaineers investing in a pair of insulated plastic boots will do well to remember that a slightly loose-fitting pair is no bad thing at very high altitudes. A closer-fitting boot, which might be excellent from a technical point-of-view, is likely to impair blood-flow in the feet and so increase the risk of frostbite. *Suggested kit lists for Kilimanjaro, Denali and 6000m peaks in the Himalaya and Karakoram are included in Appendix C.*

> ❛Use a kit list. That way you won't forget much. Even I have one!❜
>
> *John Barry*

SLEEPING BAGS

Trekkers and climbers usually want their sleeping bags to function across a wide temperature range. There are several ways to achieve this: one approach is to buy a bag designed to keep you warm in the lowest temperature you expect to encounter. The disadvantage of this method is that most of the time you will end up with a bag which is much warmer and heavier than is necessary. Another tactic is to buy a bag which will keep you warm in the majority of temperatures you expect to encounter. You can then add a fleece liner (or put the sleeping bag inside a second bag) when you head for somewhere that is colder than your sleeping bag was designed to cope with. You might choose to use a lightweight silk liner, in order to keep the bag clean. Or you might get so tangled up in the liner that it isn't worth the effort.

Airing your sleeping bag regularly will maximise its efficiency

Down kernels and synthetic fibres are the two principal types of sleeping bag insulation. Down bags take their name from the fluffy kernels found at the base of the feathers of fowl, typically ducks and geese. Down is, pound for pound, warmer than any other type of insulation and feels luxurious. If properly cared for, a down bag might last 10 or more years. However, down does requires careful handling, it loses all of its insulation when wet, and it is expensive. A down bag works brilliantly in dry, cold environments like the Himalaya (except during the monsoon).

Synthetic bags are filled with polyester filaments. They are cheaper and easier to care for than down bags, and retain some insulation when wet. However, a synthetic bag will be heavier and bulkier than an equivalent down bag, and it has a shorter useful life (typically three to six years). Synthetic bags perform particularly well in damp climates such as Patagonia.

Avoid storing your sleeping bag in the supplied stuff sack when you are not travelling: compressing the bag for long periods of time inevitably shortens its serviceable life. Bags like to be stored in large cotton sacks, laid out under beds, or hung up in wardrobes.

It is not recommended to clean your bag on a regular basis, as too many washes can have a detrimental effect on its performance. When you eventually decide that your bag needs a clean, you can do this yourself by using a proprietary cleaner or you can have a down bag professionally cleaned. If you clean a down bag yourself, bear in mind that the process takes a couple of days, and must be done with great care in order to avoid damaging the sleeping bag's internal construction. Never have any bag dry-cleaned, as the toxins used in the cleaning process damage the insulation and may also have a detrimental affect on your health. *Appendix A includes addresses of companies that offer professional cleaning services for sleeping bags.*

Sleeping bags are temperature-rated by their manufacturer, but since these ratings do not conform to an industry-wide measurement scale, they can be taken only as a guide. The overall warmth of the bag depends on many things including the grade of the filling used, the condition and age of the bag and how warm the individual is when entering the bag.

Bivouac (Bivi) Bags

Many sleeping bags now come with water-resistant outers that are quite adequate for warding off tea spills, the odd snow flurry and the dampness that accumulates overnight in a tent. However, it's essential to put your sleeping bag inside a bivouac bag if you plan to sleep outside in wet conditions without a tent or tarp. Commonly known as a 'bivi bag', bivouac bags are made from fabrics similar to those used in waterproof/breathable garments. Designs vary from models that sport a simple drawcord hood to multiple zip creations with storm flaps and tie-in points.

There are a number of bivi tents on the market that are essentially a bivi bag with a tiny hoop at one or both ends. These serve to increase the living space. It is worth noting that the weight of these hybrids is not much less than a regular lightweight tent, although a bivi tent's low profile makes it more resistant to strong winds than a taller abode.

Sleeping Mats

Sleeping bags require a foam mat to be used under them, in order to replicate the filling that is crushed when you lie down. Mats are made from closed-cell foam (low-cost and nearly indestructible) or vacuum-sealed open-cell foam (self-inflating and comfortable). If you are joining a trekking holiday and are told that mats will be supplied, beware: some companies supply mattresses that squash down to nothing when laid upon.

Getting The Most From Your Sleeping Bag

If you find yourself becoming cold during the night, there are several things you can do to remain as warm as possible.

- Unless you are in a 'survival' situation, wearing a set of dry base layer clothing – or no clothes at all – in your bag will make you feel warmer than if you had gone to bed bundled in fleece. This is because clothing serves to slow down the speed at which the heat from your body reaches the sleeping bag's insulation. Instead, place your clothes between the mat and bag. This will help to prevent the cold ground from robbing you of heat (a process known as 'cold strike').

- Folding your sleeping mat in half will double the thickness of foam under your head and torso, and further reduce cold strike. An empty rucksack can be turned into a makeshift mat for the legs and feet.

- Wear dry gloves, socks and a hat to protect your extremities. A hat is particularly important as a large percentage of body heat is lost through the head. If you can bear it, wear a balaclava or face mask too.

- Employ all the adjustments on your sleeping bag: check the entry zip is done up and secure; pull the head and neck drawcords snug against your face so only your nose and mouth protrude (to minimise the amount of condensed breath in your sleeping bag); adjust the shoulder baffle so that it sits flush around the base of your neck.

- Going to bed with a full stomach allows your body to heat a sleeping bag rapidly. Better still, eat your main meal whilst sitting in your bag. Making a hot drink in the middle of the night is a fast way to restore heat to the core. It's worth remembering that it is easier to cool a hot body than warm a chilled one.

- Take a pee bottle to bed. (Women may find a funnel a useful accessory.) Be sure to empty it straightaway, otherwise you might have a bottle of frozen urine in the morning. If you put up with a bursting bladder, the night will feel much colder, because the body will be forced to divert precious heat to the bladder to keep the liquid at a manageable temperature. Even without a bottle, you'll be better off if you get up to relieve yourself.

- Joining a pair of sleeping bags together and sharing the combined heat output of two bodies will certainly increase your overall warmth.

> Rucksack compression straps can be annoyingly short when it comes to stowing gear like sleeping mats. You can extend their length with extra pieces of webbing and tape knots.
>
> *Seb Mankelow*

Your stove will perform more efficiently if you pre-filter the fuel

STOVES

For the independent trekker or climber, a stove is a critical piece of equipment. There are two principal types of stove: pressurised and unpressurised.

Pressurised stoves create more heat and work more efficiently at altitude than unpressurised models. However, most pressurised stoves (except those that run on bottled gas) require regular maintenance. Some pressurised liquid fuel stoves which run on more than one type of fuel are known as 'multi-fuel stoves'. If you choose to take a pressurised liquid fuel stove, make sure that the fuel line can be removed and cleaned, and pack plenty of spares, especially fuel jets and jet 'prickers'. By contrast, unpressurised stoves require very little care and attention.

Since the availability of fuel will often determine the type of stove you pack, take care to find out which fuels will be available in the country you are visiting.

Cooking is dealt with in Chapter 9.

TENTS

There is an enormous number of tent designs on the market. Answering the following questions will help you to narrow down the choice:

- How many people does the tent need to accommodate?
- How much weight am I prepared to carry?
- What sort of conditions do I expect to encounter?

Built-in insect netting and a sewn-in groundsheet are two features to look for. Groundsheets are expensive to repair or replace so a secondary groundsheet (made from plastic or nylon) can be a good idea when camping on rough terrain. If you are planning to live in your tent for more than a few days at a time, then it's worth remembering that two entrances make cooking and storing gear more straightforward. Double entrances also increase the through-flow of air on a sultry night. If you are tall, be sure to check out the length of the inner tent.

Tents are pitched either flysheet-first or inner-first. Flysheet-first has the advantage of keeping the inner tent dry if you pitch the tent in the rain. Inner-first tents require the inner to go up before the flysheet. Although the

STOVE FUEL COMPARISON CHART

FUEL: Paraffin/kerosene
TYPE OF STOVE: pressurised liquid fuel
EASILY AVAILABLE IN: Asia, Africa, Himalaya
PROS: cheap and easily available, even in rural communities;
                       efficient up to 6500m
CONS: stove requires priming; fuel line clogs quickly if not
                       cleaned; messy; fuel easily taints food

FUEL: Petrol/unleaded petrol/benzine
TYPE OF STOVE: pressurised liquid fuel
EASILY AVAILABLE IN: almost everywhere that has access to motorised transport
PROS: widely available; cheaper than white gas; efficient up to 6500m
CONS: stove requires priming; fuel line clogs quickly if not cleaned

FUEL: White gas/Coleman Fuel/benzina blanca
TYPE OF STOVE: pressurised liquid fuel
EASILY AVAILABLE IN: North America, UK, benzina blanca becoming increasingly available in
                       South America
PROS: clean, so doesn't clog fuel lines as quickly as paraffin or petrol;
                       efficient up to 6500m
CONS: stove requires priming; fuel more expensive than regular petrol

FUEL: Butane or propane
TYPE OF STOVE: pressurised bottled gas
EASILY AVAILABLE IN: Europe, North America and certain other popular trekking regions
PROS: clean; hassle-free; propane/butane mix burns efficiently at all
                       altitudes and in cold weather
CONS: heavy; several different types of connection produced so
                       compatibility with stove not guaranteed; empty cartridges
                       must be disposed of carefully; butane-only mix performs
                       poorly in sub-zero temperatures

FUEL: Alcohol/methylated spirits/ethanol/alcool á brûler
TYPE OF STOVE: unpressurised liquid fuel
EASILY AVAILABLE IN: Europe, Scandinavia, North America
PROS: evaporates quickly if spilt
CONS: expensive; burns quickly; low heat output; performs
                       poorly above 3000m; some fuels are transparent so difficult to
                       see flame – take extra care when re-filling to ensure flames have
                       been completely extinguished

FUEL: Solid fuel (e.g. Hexamine)
TYPE OF STOVE: unpressurised, uncontrollable
EASILY AVAILABLE IN: Europe, North America (especially military units)
PROS: easy to light in any weather; can be used to 'prime' other stoves
CONS: very low heat output; uncontrollable flame; fumes often
                       poisonous so only use in extremely well-ventilated areas

Skis and snowshoes can make travel on snow an enjoyable experience

inner might get damp whilst the tent is being erected, the advantage of the inner-first method is that the inner is kept drum-tight by the poles to create a large living space. By contrast, outer-first tents require the inner tent to be hung inside. This method means that in windy conditions the inner might repeatedly touch the outer, allowing water to pass through to the living area by osmosis.

As a general rule, fibreglass poles are supplied with tents designed to be pitched on sheltered valley sites, whilst aluminium poles are supplied with tents built to withstand high winds on exposed mountainsides.

OTHER ITEMS OF EQUIPMENT

Eye protection in bright conditions is essential. An appropriate pair of glasses will filter out invisible ultra-violet (UV) rays. Certain models have a 'wraparound' design to protect the peripheral vision, whilst others have fixed or removable leather side-pieces. This peripheral protection is only really necessary if you are planning to encounter snow or glacial conditions, where reflected light from the surface can enter through the side of the eyewear. Goggles are the sometimes used by mountaineers and skiers.

In the mountains, a headtorch – which keeps the hands free if you have to climb, trek or visit the loo in the night – wins hands-down over all other types of illumination.

> ❛A ski stick (without the wrist strap) in one hand and an ice axe in the other is a great system for the majority of easy climbs; the pole saves your back from becoming too strained.❜
>
> *Smiler Cuthbertson*

Trekking poles are becoming increasingly popular. Converts swear by their ability to transfer some of the load from the knees, although perhaps at some cost to elbow joints (unless shock-absorbing models are used). Poles are also valuable aids when crossing rivers and negotiating difficult terrain. Detractors argue that poles are yet another piece of equipment to carry.

Water bottles are discussed in Chapter 9.

If you are planning to undertake a climb rather than a trek, it is likely that you will already have the experience to undertake the planned ascent, and probably the equipment to go with it. If you don't already own the gear, or find yourself with an unexpected opportunity to make an ascent but without the necessary hardware, you might find that the town located closest to the mountain has a rental service. This is certainly the case in places such as Huaraz in Peru. If you are part of a commercial trip, you might be able to rent some of the gear from the company that is organising your trip.

If you are tempted to hire items such as ropes, harnesses, helmets, karabiners or other climbing hardware, bear in mind that it will be impossible to ascertain whether they are in a usable state. Are you planning to use crampons? If so, ensure that your boots and crampons are compatible. *Appendix E includes a list of books that contain detailed information on climbing equipment.*

RUCKSACKS & HOLDALLS

Ideally your rucksack will be your final purchase, as only at this stage are you likely to know how much gear needs to be packed in it. If you are trekking independently, you will want to buy a rucksack that comfortably holds all of your equipment, with room to spare. This extra space will be quickly filled by food or by the equipment itself if it gets wet.

The fit of the rucksack is all-important; the aim is to transfer as much of the load from the shoulders to the stronger thigh muscles. This can be achieved by ensuring that the distance between the shoulder straps and hip belt is the same as between your shoulders and hip bone. When trying on a rucksack, make sure that some weight is put into it; all rucksacks feel comfortable when they are empty. Make sure that you can return the rucksack if it is in an unmarked condition. Then you can then load it up with all your gear, and walk around your local park for an hour or two to ensure that it is comfortable.

Once you have found a carrying system that suits the contours of your back, you can start to consider whether you want single, double, or even treble compartments. Then you'll have to choose between side pockets, expandable side pockets or no pockets at all. Many rucksack features look great in the shop when the rucksack is shiny and new, but additional zips mean more potential weak points, whilst extra pockets provides quick access to your belongings for the opportunistic thief. Check the diameter of the access hole at the top of the rucksack; some are ridiculously small, which makes packing and unpacking unnecessarily time-consuming. Only a few rucksacks on the market are guaranteed to be waterproof, so most experienced trekkers line the inside of their rucksacks with strong plastic or waterproof nylon bags. The perfect rucksack will weigh no more than 10% of the total weight you anticipate carrying.

So-called 'convertible rucksacks' – that transform from a rucksack to a regular piece of travel luggage thanks to a fabric panel that 'hides' the back

'Large cargo bags can accommodate rucksacks safely and securely, and are easy to use on all modes of transport from mules to planes.'

Jerry Gore

system when not required – are popular with travellers who only venture into the hills on an infrequent basis. Such luggage does allow the owner to enter upmarket establishments in more style than the backpacker shouldering a traditional rucksack. Another big draw of this type of hybrid design is the detachable satellite daysack that many models come with. However, the all-round zip design of the convertible rucksack is not ideal if you are trying to pack an evenly-balanced, heavy load for trekking or mountaineering. If you are going to use your rucksack for trekking more than 30% of the time, it might be wise to buy a regular rucksack.

If you are planning to join an organised expedition with attendant staff and pack animals, then a daysack (that is large enough to carry a torch, camera, first aid kit, water and food) is all that is required. It is always worth packing a second warm jumper or duvet jacket in your daysack in case you arrive at the campsite an hour or two before your equipment. Also, make sure that you carry your valuables or fragile items in order to save embarrassment all round if an item breaks or goes missing. All your other gear can go in a holdall, which is then transported by a porter, yak or mule. It is really not worth investing in an expensive, fully-adjustable rucksack just for this gear, as the porter will probably carry it with a strop that goes around his forehead, or simply balance it on top of his head. So much for all that research and development on rucksack carrying systems!

Packing Your Rucksack

The order in which you pack your belongings into the rucksack very much depends on the activity you are engaged in. Long-distance walkers following well-established trails with only gentle gradients often pile heavy items into the top third of their rucksacks. This 'top-heavy' approach would not necessarily suit the trekker moving across awkward ground, who is more likely to favour slotting the heaviest pieces of equipment down the back of the rucksack. Packing this way keeps the weight of the rucksack close to the spinal column and maintains the natural centre of gravity.

It is wise to let the mantra, 'first in, last out' be your guide. One loading sequence for backpackers carrying all their own equipment is described here; after a day or two you will no doubt discover your own order.

- Base: spare clothes and sleeping bag in a separate waterproof bag
- Centre: food, cooking equipment, medical kit, torch
- Top: tent, warm jumper, hat, gloves, money and paperwork
- Top pocket: map, camera film, water purification tablets, suncream, sunglasses

- Side pockets: water, fuel, snacks (keep fuel separate)
- Between waterproof liner and rucksack: waterproofs, gaiters
- Outside: tent poles, sleeping mat, umbrella, camera

Packing the tent near the top of your load will allow you to erect your shelter in wet weather without having to empty your rucksack. Try to minimise the number of items left dangling on the outside of your rucksack so that nothing can fall off.

Meeting Luggage Restrictions On Flights

Even after you have pared down your equipment to the bare minimum, it can sometimes be difficult to meet an airline's weight allowance (except on flights to the USA which operate a two-piece luggage system). Traditionally, travellers circumvented this problem by squeezing a terrific amount of heavy equipment into their hand luggage. However, it is increasingly common for this luggage to be weighed if you take it up to the check-in desk with you. So some people wear their bulky outdoor clothing and footwear onto the aircraft: once on board, the excess gear is bundled into an overhead locker. Although only one piece of hand luggage is officially allowed in the aircraft cabin, a small waist pack is normally overlooked. At all times, bear in mind the small size of overhead lockers, and ensure that the hand baggage you take on board is small enough to meet the airline's requirements.

Note that ice axes and all knives (including penknives) should be packed inside checked-in luggage. It is illegal to carry lighters and fuel in your luggage. Mountain travellers usually buy fuel on arrival, whilst some expeditions ship gas canisters in advance.

WHERE TO GO TO GET MORE ADVICE

If you have never bought any outdoor equipment before, don't worry: there are plenty of sources of information to help you make an informed choice.

Reading the gear review and advice pages of outdoor magazines and websites can be a good starting point. Bear in mind that reviewers often have only a short period of time to assess a product. Only a few publications do long-term tests, as by the time such a review has been published, the manufacturer is likely to have changed the product's specification. Brochures from manufacturers and retailers are useful for checking the specification of individual products, but try and avoid being sucked in by the glamorous copy written about each item.

When it comes to choosing an outdoor retailer, attempt to find one that has a wide range of products from several manufacturers. In the event that the merchandise you want is out-of-stock or discontinued, they will be in a position to suggest an alternative. It is also worth enquiring as to whether the sales staff work on commission. Staff on fixed salaries are perhaps more likely to offer impartial advice. Maybe one of the company's employees has been to the destination that you are travelling to? First-hand advice based on personal experience is invaluable. If you find a member of staff who gives impartial advice, and who is prepared to suggest a particular product even if his shop does not sell it, then hold onto that person: even if the store he works in is slightly more expensive than its competitors, this level of expertise is likely to save you money in the long run as you will be steered away from making purchases of unnecessary equipment.

Some of the best advice can be obtained freely from other outdoor users, many of whom enjoy talking about their gear both in person and via outdoor websites. You are unlikely to find two people who have the same opinion about any one piece of equipment – even if they both own the same item – which may add clarity or yet more chaos to your final decision. Everyone, from reviewer to user, is naturally biased to some degree. In no time at all you will find yourself as opinionated as the next person.

SAVING MONEY ON GEAR

If you are setting out on your first trek and don't want to splash all your cash on an activity that you're not sure you are going to enjoy, have a good look through your wardrobe. Perhaps you have a polyester t-shirt that might serve as a base layer? Or a wool jumper for a mid-layer? An old windproof rowing cagoule will serve quite admirably as an outer layer on many treks that take place in the dry season, especially if you double it up with a lightweight umbrella. If you are on a trek that is employing porters, a sports dufflebag will prove more than satisfactory as a holder for your sleeping bag and spare clothing: important items such as your sleeping bag can be waterproofed inside a bin liner. Or you may be able to persuade a keen hillwalking friend to lend you their old gear. When it comes to buying new equipment, think about what you will use most. For example, a waterproof jacket is likely to get used far more than a pair of waterproof overtrousers.

KNOW YOUR GEAR

Once you have obtained all your equipment, it is important to test every item thoroughly before departure; no-one wants a critical piece of equipment to let them down in a place where a replacement cannot be readily sought. If this means a night of camping out in your garden, then so be it! Knowing how to pitch your tent in the dark, adjust the back length of your rucksack on the move and clean your stove in just a few minutes are invaluable skills that are best learnt in comfortable surroundings.

YOUR QUESTIONS ANSWERED

How much gear should I take?

Whether you are travelling independently or joining a commercial trek or climb, it is always a good idea to minimise the amount of gear that you take. If you have bought wisely and invested in apparel that can perform over a wide temperature range in a variety of conditions, you will probably find that a set of outer clothing, two base layers (one to wear and one to wash), one or two mid-layers (the number and thickness will be determined by where you are going) and two or three sets of socks will prove sufficient for most trips lasting up to a month. Overall weight can also be minimised by taking one wash kit, one medical kit, one guidebook and a single set of maps between two or more people. Solo trekkers will have to carry all of these items on their own. *Appendix C contains suggested kit lists for a variety of destinations.*

14

> 'Allow for the 'cock-up' factor in everything – costs, timings, rendezvous, porters, route finding and pick-ups.'

John Barry

International Rescue

EMERGENCIES

A medical emergency in the mountains calls for a cool head and prompt action. Common sense is as important as medical knowledge. Try to remain calm. Take stock of what has happened and of any other people who are around. Make good use of competent individuals: try to avoid doing everything yourself. After first aid has been administered (preferably by a trained person), get hold of the victim's passport. Attempting to leave the country without it will be very difficult.

The next thing to think about is summoning assistance. Depending on the severity of the injury or illness, this might involve sending a request to the nearest village for people to help carry the casualty. Or it might require getting word to the victim's medical assistance company or embassy in order to effect a professional land-based or aeromedical evacuation. As well as details of the casualty, the authorities are going to require details of your location. Ideally, mark this on your map and write down in plain words the details of what has happened, as well as other relevant information such as the size and overall condition of the rest of the team.

You will need to decide whether to remain where the accident occurred or move to another location with the whole party. Your decision is likely to be influenced by a number of factors including:

- Any further danger imposed by the immediate environment
- The amount of clothing, shelter, medical supplies and food you have
- The severity of the victim's injury

If you do decide to move, then draw on the map the direction you are heading in. Rescuers will then know where to start searching if you are not at the site of the accident when they arrive. Give this information to the person who is being despatched to summon help. The nearest telephone might be days or even weeks away, but however far it is, try to ensure that someone (preferably the person you sent with the original request) returns to tell you that the request for a rescue has been successfully put through to an appropriate authority. Having access to a communication device in this type of situation could prove to be invaluable. *You can read about different types of communication devices later in this chapter.*

In some countries, a rescue may not be launched until payment for it has been guaranteed. If you are travelling with a commercial operator, make sure that they have a bond to cover such eventualities and give your insurance details to the group leader. If you are travelling on your own, it is wise to leave a copy of your insurance policy and passport number with your embassy on arrival in-country. Your embassy will probably be the first organisation that the rescue authorities will contact. In an emergency situation in a remote location, a wad of dollars can be the fastest way to make things happen.

Whilst you are waiting for support, keep a written record of the patient's condition. If you did not see the accident take place, try and collect an eye-witness account. This will help the medical authorities determine what treatment to administer to the patient.

Helicopter Rescue

If a helicopter is sent, you will need to consider a landing area for it. The ideal landing pad will be clearly marked with a bright piece of material that is securely weighed or tied down. Make sure there are no other pieces of clothing and equipment lying around. A flying sleeping bag could endanger the safety of the helicopter. Check the angle and firmness of the terrain. Small rescue helicopters require an open area of at least 20 metres in diameter that is clear of cliffs, trees and pylons. The larger the landing area, the more chance the helicopter has of coming in to rescue you. If you have time, think about the direction that the helicopter will come into land. Pilots prefer to land or hover into wind. Is the approach also clear of all obstructions?

When the helicopter lands, do not jump up and run towards it. Rotor and tail blades are deadly. Wait for the winchman to get out and come to you, or watch for the pilot to signal for you to approach. If directed to approach, only do so from the front-quarter (i.e. towards the pilot). If a landing is impossible, a winch rescue may be feasible. In these instances, keep clear of the descending winch or winchman until the cable comes to the ground, as a static electrical discharge may occur. Do exactly as the winchman commands. Declare any pyrotechnics (such as flares) you are carrying to the winchman so that they can be dealt with in the appropriate manner (it is likely that they will be left behind). It is possible that the winchman will put a strop around your body. If so, do not raise your arms above your head as you are winched towards the door of the helicopter, or you might slip out of the strop with potentially fatal consequences. Remain passive, and allow the winch operator to manhandle you into the machine.

Helicopters are sometimes sent out to look for people who have been reported as missing. If you see a helicopter and require assistance, do everything you can to attract attention. Create a smoky fire by day, and a regular fire by night. Lay brightly-coloured items out on dark-coloured rocks or snow. A mirror or another reflective object (such as a CD) can be used to deflect light towards the aircraft. At night, a torch can be used. Launch flares if you have them, but do not aim them at the helicopter. When you are seen, stand with arms raised to create a 'Y' position, which will tell the pilot, "Yes, I need help". If you are 'buzzed' by a helicopter but do not require assistance, raise one arm and lower the other in order to create the diagonal part of the letter 'N'. This will tell the pilot, "No, I do not need help."

In-Country Medical Treatment

Once the patient has been rescued, he will probably end up in a local medical centre. In a developing country, such a facility may be abysmal. If injections or intravenous (IV) fluids need to be given, make sure that the staff use your sterile medical kit. Needles in certain countries' health centres are sometimes shared: such a practice increases the risk of transmitting disease. Do not allow a blood transfusion to take place unless it is a matter of life and death, as a blood screening programme may not be in place. *Appendix D includes a list of items for a sterile medical kit.*

Repatriation

Get in touch with your medical assistance company to arrange for repatriation, or an evacuation to the nearest 'centre of medical excellence'. However, bear in mind that some injuries can be made worse if the patient is moved.

‘ Emergency procedures must take into account any special provision for the disabled team member. I've been witness to trips where not only has the disabled person been put at risk through a lack of equipment, capability and back-up but the able-bodied people have placed themselves at risk because they ended up stretching their own skills beyond their limits. ’

Glenn Shaw

Fatalities

In the event of a fatality, the main decision is likely to be whether or not to have the body repatriated. Just getting the body to an international airport may prove very difficult. Depending on the cause of death, and the country the body is being returned to, the body may have to be embalmed or cremated. Try to arrange to have the body photographed so that there is no subsequent doubt in the minds of the people back home as to the identity of the deceased. If a decision is made not to repatriate the body, or if the body is unrecoverable, try and have any memorial service documented.

COMMUNICATION SYSTEMS

Communication devices that are of interest to expeditions and independent travellers fall into two broad categories; long-range communication with the outside world and short-range communication between members of the party. Whilst very high frequency (VHF) handheld radios are quite cheap and straightforward to use, long-range radios are expensive and usually require specialist training. Unsurprisingly, mobile satellite telephony has recently become an attractive option for some people. The communications industry is a rapidly advancing one and it is likely that new technologies will have appeared on the market by the time you read this.

Do You Need To Establish Communications?

Traditionally, remote communications were only of practical interest to large expeditions. Today, the advent of handheld satellite telephones and realistic call charges has encouraged a small but increasing number of expeditions, as well as individual mountain travellers, to set out with their own link to the outside world.

Being able to call for assistance in an emergency is the main reason why individuals and expeditions include communication devices as part of their equipment. However, with this ability to call for help comes a responsibility not to abuse the medium. Being able to summon a helicopter or rescue team should not prevent you from taking every possible precaution to prevent an incident occurring and to self-rescue if an accident does happen. Even if you are able to speak directly to the rescue authorities (assuming such an organisation exists in the country) there is no guarantee that a rescue attempt will be mounted. If a helicopter is despatched, poor weather conditions or the altitude you are at may prevent it from being able to reach you. It is wise not to rely solely on a single piece of communication technology if contact with the outside world is essential; the mountain

environment can quickly take its toll on electronic equipment, regardless of
whether the product has been designed to withstand rain and shock.
Moisture, sand and dirt can all work their way into delicate apparatus.
Animals may try to eat the cables and insects can short-out circuit boards.
Materials may snap in the cold and melt in the heat. Equipment has been
known to be struck by lightning and people can break even the most
well-made products. It is suggested that communication equipment is
carried in a waterproof, dustproof and foam-lined plastic box that is capable
of withstanding sustained abuse.

Which Communication Device Is Right For You?

Answering the following questions might help you to make an informed
decision about which type of device is likely to meet your requirements:

- Where in the world are you communicating from?
- How regularly do you want to communicate and with whom?
- Which systems are authorised for use in the country you are visiting?
- Which systems physically work at the altitude and latitude you are visiting?

Rather than describing individual systems, this section explains the advantages and disadvantages of the generic types of communication (land-based, radio, cellular and satellite) that are currently available and which may be of interest to certain independent trekkers, small groups or larger expeditions. Between them, the options outlined here cover voice, fax, pager and email. A team that wants or needs to send large amounts of data (such as digital photographs or video footage) will need to consider a more powerful system than those described below. *Appendix A includes a list of communication technology providers.*

Land-Based

An increasing number of towns and villages in remote regions are beginning to be equipped with telephones. If your expedition is operating within range of such settlements, then it might be possible to use a land-line facility for emergency or regular communication. Access to a reliable land-line may allow you to send and receive electronic data more efficiently than by cellular or satellite telephone. However, maintenance of these land-lines may be irregular; some lines have been known to break down regularly for days or even weeks.

Radio

Two-way radios are useful for both short and long distance communication. The transmitting range of small and inexpensive handheld radios depends upon their power output and the terrain across or through which the signal must travel. For instance, a person talking from the summit of one mountain to a person standing on the summit of another peak is likely to enjoy a better reception than two people the same distance away who are trying to communicate from the depths of steep-sided valleys. That said, some two-way radio users have succeeded in 'bouncing' their transmissions off valley walls in order to extend the effective range of their walkie-talkies. VHF radio performance can be greatly enhanced if a powerful base station radio is used. Simply raising the height of the base station antenna will also improve reception.

Long-range radios need a member of the team to be 'listening out' on the other end, so it vital to arrange transmission schedules in advance, together

with a contingency plan if communication has not been established after a certain period of time. With the correct equipment and knowledge about how long-range radio works, it is possible to communicate over a distance of several thousand kilometres.

A third type of radio transmitter, that is often favoured as an emergency back-up to other forms of communication, is commonly known as an Emergency Position Indicating Radio Beacon (EPIRB) or a Personal Locator Beacon (PLB). EPIRBs and PLBs are small, self-contained radio transmitters which can be activated to alert rescue authorities to an emergency. They transmit a signal on one of several international distress frequencies which can be picked up by either passing aircraft or the COSPAS-SARSAT satellite system. This information is then relayed to the nearest rescue co-ordination centre to where the emergency signal originated. This type of radio does not allow for two-way communication so it is not possible to explain the nature of the emergency.

There are two main types of EPIRB/PLB. The less sophisticated version operates in the 121.5/243 MHz range. The satellite coverage of this type will be phased out by 2009 in favour of the more advanced 406 MHz transmitters which have a unique ID code registered to the owner. If you decide to use a 406 MHz model it is important to find out what the procedure is if you activate the beacon. By contrast, owners of 121.5/243 MHz beacons need to be aware that in certain parts of the world little or no action is taken if this type of beacon is detected: if you decide to rely on a 121.5/243 MHz transmitter be sure to inform the police in the nearest administrative centre that you are carrying one.

Cellular

Cellular phones work by sending and receiving voice and data through a network of cells that are usually mounted on buildings and towers. Unsurprisingly, most mountainous regions are not covered. In developing countries, cellular coverage may be completely non-existent. If you know that the area you are travelling to has cellular coverage, make sure that your mobile phone can be used: you are advised to contact your network provider before departure in order to check that permission to use your telephone abroad has been activated. This service is usually known as 'roaming'. You may need a telephone that has the ability to work on dual or triple bandwidths. Cellular calls made from abroad can sometimes be more expensive than those made from a satellite telephone.

Satellite

Satellite communication systems are now well-established. Portable units range from briefcase-sized devices weighing a couple of kilos to handheld units that are slightly larger than cellular phones. It is the latter type that has the potential to revolutionise remote communication for independent travellers and lightweight expeditions. There are several satellite constellations currently in operation. The network that you choose to align yourself with will depend on several factors, including whether you want voice, fax, pager or data services. The cost per minute of incoming as well as outgoing calls should also be borne in mind. Certain constellations maintain a near-constant level of communication ability. Other systems can only 'speak' to the satellite as it passes overhead at certain times of day. If you are using a lightweight or handheld satellite system to broadcast data (such as email) it is likely that transmission speed will be painfully slow. It is suggested that you keep the length and number of email messages to a minimum in case the call is 'dropped' by the satellite during transmission.

Establishing A Communication System

Establishing communication with the outside world is not always easy. All types of communication (except cable systems) work best if they can 'see' the medium that they need to communicate with. In the case of radio and satellite communication, this means the sky. An expedition broadcasting from an open plain or mountain top with a distant view of the horizon in all directions will be able to establish contact with the outside world more easily than a team speaking from the base of a narrow valley or from beneath trees. In addition to being able to physically transmit, most types of communication devices need a license before they can be used legally. In the case of satellite communication, this permit is normally negotiated by the owners of the constellation. When it comes to radios, you might have to apply for a license to transmit on a designated frequency.

POWER

Communication systems can use large amounts of power, so it is worth thinking about what power sources you are going to rely upon during the expedition. Re-chargeable batteries can be connected to solar cells, whilst custom-made single-use alkaline or lithium batteries may be configured to fit existing products. A single-use battery will normally provide more power than a re-chargeable, making it ideal for emergency use. AA battery packs are available for several types of radios and many expeditions have found this option to be more convenient than the re-charging approach. Larger expeditions have experimented with small liquid fuel generators (although these often perform poorly at high altitude), and even small wind turbines.

PROS AND CONS OF DIFFERENT BATTERIES

Lithium Battery

+ Holds a charge in hot weather
+ Stores around three times more power than an equivalent NiCad or NiMH battery

- Can be reluctant to take a charge in cold weather
- Intolerant of power fluctuations so must be re-charged precisely: always use the supplied charger between the power supply (such as a solar panel)and battery

NiCad or NiMH Battery

+ Tolerant of power fluctuations
+ Can be connected directly to a solar panel

- Self-discharges rapidly in hot weather
- Stores much less power than the equivalent weight lithium battery

Optimising Battery Life

If you do decide to take modern technology into the mountains, bear in mind that consumer batteries are designed to work in ambient temperatures of between 15-25°C. Try to re-create this environment as best you can. In cold weather this will probably require you to warm the battery up next to the body before placing it on the device or the charger. You might also have to rotate two or three batteries at any one time. In hot weather (and remember that tents can become ferociously hot) try to keep equipment cool.

When a NiCad or NiMH battery is fully charged it loses excess power by warming itself up. However in cold weather this heating process (known as re-combination) cannot take place. This leads to a build-up of pressure within the battery which if left unchecked will result in a catastrophic failure. Re-charging these types of batteries inside a tent or somewhere relatively warm will allow re-combination to take place.

In extremes of temperatures don't expect miracles. Anticipate a substantial shortfall in power of between 60-70% of the battery's capability. Take plenty of cells, and think seriously about purchasing larger-capacity batteries if they are available. It might prove possible to purchase a one-use alkaline battery for items like camcorders and mobile phones. Alkalines store a lot more energy than rechargeable batteries. So if all else fails you can fall back on this as a reserve.

If you are heading straight into a cold environment it's sensible to charge batteries before departure. If you're going to be arriving in a hot climate leave the batteries flat and charge them a couple of hours before use. The reason for this is simple: over a period of four weeks a battery will lose around 80% of its power in a temperature of 40°C. One word of warning: if batteries are abused they can fail, leak and even catch fire. Be alert to this danger, especially in cold weather when you might be keeping batteries close to your skin or in a sleeping bag.

THE GLOBAL POSITIONING SYSTEM (GPS)
How The System Works

The American GPS system consists of 24 satellites that bathe the Earth in accurate time signals. (Competing systems are expected to become available). Each satellite also sends out a unique code. When a handheld GPS receiving unit is turned on it searches the sky, hunting for satellites.

When a satellite is seen and identified, the handheld unit can work out where in the world it is – latitude, longitude and altitude – by checking the time delay between when the signal was sent and received. It should be noted that because of the way that a satellite 'looks down' on the Earth, the altitude reading will rarely be as accurate as the latitude and longitude. By locking on to an increasing number of satellites, a more accurate 'fix' can be established by the handheld unit, using a similar process to triangulation.

Once the handheld GPS unit knows where it is, the direction and distance to other co-ordinates (such as summits, valley bases, bridges and huts) can be computed. This information is displayed on a screen that identifies where you are in relation to your waypoint, and a navigation cursor that indicates the direction and distance to a given destination. Most GPS devices are able to store your route as you progress.

In foul weather a GPS can be a useful aid to navigation but it does not replace the compass

Access to a GPS receiver means that in an emergency you will be able to give your exact position (in latitude and longitude) to the rescue authorities. A GPS and satellite telephone can reduce the time it takes to be rescued from days or weeks to mere hours, assuming that both devices are functioning correctly, and that weather conditions allow the helicopter to reach you.

YOUR QUESTIONS ANSWERED

Does a GPS mean I don't have to bother with a map or compass?

Over-reliance on GPS is not recommended for several reasons. Batteries and electronic components can fail, so it is essential that the user is able to navigate with a map and compass when necessary. The altitude reading on a handheld GPS unit is unlikely to be as accurate as a correctly calibrated altimeter, so in certain circumstances – such as descending a narrow arête in poor visibility – using the GPS for guidance is unwise.

Bear in mind that at any moment the US Government is able to render the GPS inaccurate to 100 metres or more, rather than the usual accuracy which may be 10 metres or less. Navigating when the system is downgraded in this way could be dangerous, particularly in bad weather. It should also be noted that GPS performance is adversely affected when the handheld unit cannot 'see' a large portion of the sky.

15

WELCOME TO THE BETTER
ACCLIMATIZATION CENTER
THE "REFUGIO PERÙ" CAMPO 2 PISCO 4765 mt.
FACILITIES:
• STONE-REFUGE WITH 80 BEDS.
• BATHROOMS AND HOT SHOWER
• HOT-MEAL SERVICE BREAKFAST LUNCH DIN-NER
• EXCELLENT LOCATION FOR CLIMBING, ...
  TREKKING... (beautiful scenary)
  5 OR 7 HOURS TO SUMMIT OF NEVA-
  DO PISCO (5752 mts)
• EMERGENCY RADIO SERVICE IN
  COTTAGE . FIRST-AID
  (FACILITIES WITH PERMANENT
  IN-HOUSE NURSE)-
• VERY ECONOMIC PRICES...
  WE WAIT FOR YOU
                        SOON!
(PERUVIAN AND ITALIAN
                        FOOD)

> First-time trekkers often give away pens and sweets indiscriminately to young children who have done nothing to deserve them. It is far better to make such gifts to their schoolteacher, who can then give them out as rewards for good work.

George Band

Giving Something Back

For all its negative effects, mountain tourism has the potential to bring money to impoverished areas. Used wisely, this cash can improve things like education, medical facilities, housing and water supplies for local people.

In 1960, Sir Edmund Hillary received a petition from the people of the Everest region in Nepal. It read, "Our children have eyes but cannot see, they have ears but cannot hear, can you help us to build a school in our village?" Over 40 years later and Sir Edmund Hillary's Himalayan Trust has built 28 schools, two hospitals and 13 health posts. Young people have been awarded educational scholarships, clean water systems have been installed and forestry work has been undertaken. Support for the region's monasteries has helped to strengthen the religious, cultural and community life of the local population. Together with a committee of Sherpas, Sir Edmund still tours the area every year to direct funding to the most needy projects. Local people are employed to carry out any work that is required.

Showing an interest in local people can encourage a sense of pride amongst villagers

‘ Leave the host country better off for your visit. Make a good impression, pay your bills and give something from the team – such as the medical kit – to a local hospital, or equipment to a community organisation. ’

Peter Hillary

Whilst trekkers and mountaineers who head into the mountains for the first time often think only about the famous peaks that they will see, it is not unusual for the local people who they meet to leave a stronger imprint in their memories. Like Sir Edmund, many climbers and trekkers feel a compulsion to assist these mountain people, many of whom remain cheerful and indefatigable despite little or no education, sanitation or medical facilities.

The Himalayan Trust is one of the better known mountain charities. It is a shining example of how indigenous populations can improve their situation whilst retaining ancient customs and traditions. Other aid organisations have similar goals in different mountain regions around the world; making a financial donation to such a charity is one way that the visitor returning from the mountains can make a difference.

With a little forethought, it may prove possible to make additional positive contributions as the following examples illustrate.

USING LOCALLY-RUN SERVICES

In 1994 a women's co-operative was established in the Greek village of Dadia, which lies within the boundary of the Dadia Forest Reserve in the Rhodope Mountains. The women give illustrated talks, guide tours, provide environmental information, make and sell handicrafts and cook traditional dishes for visitors. This has generated a much-needed source of supplementary income for their families. It has also helped to change local people's initial hostility towards the forest reserve which was caused by the

Will today's mountain
children leave their
communities for the
cities?

limitations placed upon logging activities. Many young people in Dadia now feel that they have a future in the area and are electing to stay rather than head for work in the cities.

Increasingly, mountain tourism is being viewed as one way – and sometimes the only way – to prevent migration from rural areas. If you so wish, every drachma, pound, rupee, peso and dollar that you spend can be used as a vote. You can choose to travel with a local or foreign trekking operator that invests in training for local people to become guides. You can stay in a lodge built and run by local people. You can even drink locally-brewed beer and enjoy local food, rather than eating a meal that looks and tastes like something you could buy at home. By voting with your wallet, you can do much to improve the lives of people in the regions that you visit.

> Local people are masters of their surroundings: they know a lot about the area, the peaks and their names, legends and customs. Talk to them on trail or at your camps, and you will return with more wealth than what only mountain views can give you.

Harish Kapadia

Learning a bit of the local language is a sure way to win new friends

BUYING HANDICRAFTS

In 1993, a non-governmental organisation called 'Handmade in America' was founded by local citizens. Its aim was to explore ways in which the Appalachian region could use its reputation as a home for some of the USA's longest-established craft organisations, to increase sales of artefacts directly to tourists. With guidance from local citizens, 'Handmade' produced a driver's guidebook to the Blue Ridge range of mountains. The guidebook had two aims: to direct people off the highway and towards local craft centres (so that the craft producers could spend more time in their workshops and less time at fairs); and to steer visitors away from sacred community places in order to help retain the cultural integrity of the region. Over 20,000 copies of the first edition were sold, and average sales have increased by 30% since publication.

It is always worth asking where attractive souvenirs come from. Are they produced in the local area? (Sometimes the underside of the item will reveal where they were produced.) Buying locally-made handicrafts for a fair price directly from the people who made them – rather than from someone at the end of a chain that began in a factory in the lowlands or another country – is just one more way to support people who are keeping mountain traditions alive.

DO YOU REALLY WANT TO GO?

Uluru, otherwise known as Ayers Rock, is one of the most famous mountains in the world. Climbing to its summit is for many visitors the highlight of their stay in Australia. Yet Uluru is a sacred mountain to the Anangu people. Because of the many injuries and deaths that occur to climbers who ascend the rock, park wardens have fixed a handrail to the summit, even though the route of ascent and the summit are regarded by the Anangu as places where their secret knowledge is discussed or stored. Now a tourist centre has been established to explain to visitors the cultural significance of Uluru. People are requested not to make the ascent. This approach seems to be working; whilst the volume of visitors remains unchanged, the number of recorded ascents is declining.

As an increasing number of people head for the mountain regions of the world, some tourists are beginning to wonder whether they should avoid certain sacred places altogether. For example, pilgrims outnumber tourists in Gangotri, in the Indian Himalaya, by 100-1: if relatively wealthy visitors continue to visit then more infrastructure is likely to be built. This in turn will further erode what remains of these important religious sites.

Perhaps it is also worth asking whether we need to visit the same place more than once? This might be a difficult issue for a mountaineer who wants to return to a peak he failed to climb on the first attempt. The same question may be easier to answer if you want to re-visit World Heritage sites such as Machu Picchu in Peru.

> ❝I can't imagine being in Tibet without my phrasebook, not just because it makes you feel you can pick up a bit of the language, but also to see the expression of joy on the faces of the Tibetans when they realise that somebody somewhere cares enough to produce a book with their language in it.❞
>
> *Nick Foxton*

YOUR QUESTIONS ANSWERED

Can I really make a difference?

It is not companies, trade organisations or governments but individuals who initiate positive change and nowhere is this more true than in the mountain environment. The individual may be an outsider or a local person. Ultimately, it is down to individual trekkers and climbers to decide what sort of mountain environments and cultures they want to experience now and in the future. Just by purchasing this book you have directly contributed to the work of the British Mountaineering Council in areas such as access and conservation. Much has recently been achieved to improve and maintain conditions in the mountains around the world. But much more remains to be done.

Appendix A: Resources

Every effort has been made to ensure that at the time of writing (autumn 2001) this information was accurate. The inclusion of any company or individual within this appendix is not an endorsement or recommendation by the author or the BMC. All addresses are in the UK unless otherwise stated.

www.thebmc.co.uk/mountaintravel.htm
The home page for this book contains additional information, web links and updates.

Advisory Organisations

The British Mountaineering Council (BMC)
177-179 Burton Road
West Didsbury
Manchester M20 2BB
tel: +44 (0)161 445 4747
fax: +44 (0)161 445 4500
email: office@thebmc.co.uk
www.thebmc.co.uk
Appendix F describes the work of the BMC.

Alpine Club of Great Britain (AC)
55 Charlotte Road
London EC2A 3QT
tel: +44 (0)20 7613 0755
fax: +44 (0)20 7613 0755
email: sec@alpine-club.org.uk
www.alpine-club.org.uk
The Alpine Club is the only UK-based mountaineering club that caters specifically for those who climb in the Alps and the Greater Ranges of the world. Active alpine climbers of any ability are invited to join. The AC promotes a code of climbing ethics which seeks to protect mountains, and mountain regions and their people, from any harmful impact by climbers.

The Mountaineering Council of Scotland
The Old Granary
West Mill St.
Perth PH1 5QP
tel: +44 (0)1738 638227
fax: +44 (0)1738 442095
email: info@mountaineering-scotland.org.uk
www.mountaineering-scotland.org.uk

Expedition Advisory Centre (EAC)
The Royal Geographical Society with the Institute of British Geographers (RGS-IBG)
1 Kensington Gore
London SW7 2AR
tel: +44 (0)20 7591 3030
fax: +44 (0)207 591 3031
email: eac@rgs.org
www.rgs.org
The catalogue of RGS-IBG expedition reports, together with details of over 7,500 planned and past expeditions, is held on a database maintained by the EAC. For a list of reports relevant to your area of interest, email the EAC or carry out your own search via their website. The EAC programme of seminars and workshops brings specialists and beginners together to provide first-hand information and training for expeditions and field researchers. The annual expedition planning seminar (held in November) is the starting point for many expeditions.

The Young Explorers' Trust (YET)
The Royal Geographical Society
1 Kensington Gore
London SW7 2AR
tel/fax: +44 (0)1623 861027
email: ted@yet2.demon.co.uk
www.yet2.demon.co.uk
The Young Explorers' Trust aims to support and assist all those involved in expeditions for young people through its extensive advice service.

The Himalayan Club
Honorary Secretary
c/o Divyesh Muni
D/18, No.155
M.I.G. Colony, Bandra East
Mumbi 400 051, India
Phones: +91 659 1837
Fax: +91 22 690 3141
email: munico@vsnl.com
www.himalayanclub.com
This club is the only international body dedicated to mountaineering in the Himalaya, Karakoram and Hindu Kush.

Safety

Foreign & Commonwealth Office (FCO)

Travel Advice Unit

Consular Section

Old Admiralty Building

London SW1A 2PA

tel: +44 (0)20 7008 0232/0233

fax: +44 (0)20 7008 0155

email: consular.fco@gtnet.gov.uk

www.fco.gov.uk/travel

Also on BBC2 Ceefax p470 onwards.

The FCO maintains up-to-date country information on circumstances affecting individuals' safety abroad.

United States Department of State Travel Advice

http://travel.state.gov/travel_warnings.html

Medical

British Airways Travel Clinic

156 Regent Street

London W1B 5LR

tel: +44 (0)20 7439 9584

fax: +44 (0)20 7287 9206

www.britishairways.com/travelclinics

A walk-in clinic; no appointment is necessary.

Medical Advisory Service for Travellers Abroad (MASTA)

Keppel Street

London WC1E 7HT

tel: +44 1276 685 040

for a printed country health brief tel: 0906 8 224100 (premium rate)

www.masta.org

Services include the supply of vaccines, travel medicines and unique products for travellers.

Nomad Travellers Store and Medical Centre

3-4 Wellington Terrace

Turnpike Lane

London N8 0PX

tel: +44 (0)20 8889 7014

travel health info line: 0906 8633414 – straight through to a nurse (premium rate)

fax: +44 (0)20 8889 9529

email: sales@nomadtravel.co.uk

www.nomadtravel.co.uk

Nomad have additional centres around the UK.

UIAA Mountain Medicine Centre

(Address and telephone number as for the BMC)

www.thebmc.co.uk/world.htm

The centre is run on a voluntary basis by Dr Charles Clarke who has a wide knowledge of the problems of high altitude and expedition medicine. The centre aims to advise climbers and mountain travellers. Specific areas of interest are covered in a series of information sheets which can be viewed on the website or requested from the BMC. The centre also offers a clinical advisory service. If a clinical opinion about a patient is required, then a referral via the GP is usually necessary.

Mountain Medicine and Traumatology Department of Chamonix Hospital (DMTM)

509 route des Pélerins

PO Box 30, Les Bossons

74400 Chamonix

France

tel: +33 (0)450 53 84 00

fax: +33 (0)450 53 84 74

email: dmtmcham@wanadoo.fr

http://perso.wanadoo.fr/dmtmcham/dmtm_uk.htm

CIWEC Clinic Travel Medicine Center

Yak & Yeti Road

Durbar Marg

PO Box 12895

Kathmandu

Nepal

tel +977 1 228531/241732

fax: +977 1 224675

email: advice@ciwec-clinic.com

www.ciwec-clinic.com

Kathmandu and Chamonix are two of the most popular destinations for mountain travellers; embassies might be able to advise on medical facilities in other areas.
Additional medical websites can be found at:
www.thebmc.co.uk/mountaintravel.htm

Portable Pressure Chambers And Oxygen Systems

Portable Altitude Chamber (PAC)
Himalayan Medical Supplies
PO Box 53, Repton
New South Wales 2454
Australia
tel: +61 2 6653 4241
fax: +61 2 6655 0266
email: pac@treksafe.com.au
www: treksafe.com.au

The Gamow Bag
Chinook Medical Gear Inc.
3455 Main Avenue
Durango, CO 81301
USA
tel: +1 970 375 1241
fax: +1 970 375 6343
email: chinook@frontier.net
www.chinookmed.com

CERTEC
Le Bourg
69210 Sourcieux-les-Mines
France
tel: +33 (0)4 74 70 39 82
fax: +33 (0)4 74 70 37 66
email: contact@certec.fr
www.certec.fr/portable_GB.html

Further information on the use of portable pressure chambers can be found at:
www.thebmc.co.uk/world/mm/mm4.htm
and www.high-altitude-medicine.com/hyperbaric.
Advice on oxygen systems for use at high altitudes can be found at: www.thebmc.co.uk/world/mm/mm8.htm

Communications

Expedition Kit Ltd
Unit 6D, Farm Lane Trading Centre
101 Farm Lane
London SW6 1QJ
tel: +44 (0)20 7610 0700
fax: +44 (0)20 7381 9769
email: sales@expeditionkit.co.uk
www.expeditionkit.co.uk
Supplier of satellite equipment to travellers and groups.

Globalstar
+1 408 933 4500
email: sales@globalstar.com
www.globalstar.com
Satellite telephone provider.

Inmarsat Ltd.
99 City Road
London EC1Y 1AX
tel: +44 (0)20 7728 1100
fax: +44 (0)20 7728 1142
email: information@inmarsat.com
www.inmarsat.com

Iridium Satellite LLC
8440 South River Parkway
Tempe, AZ 85284
USA
tel: +1 480 752 5155
email: info@iridium.com
www.iridium.com
Re-established handheld satellite telephone provider.

O'Gara Satellite Networks Ltd.
25 The Clarendon Centre
Salisbury Business Park
Salisbury
Wiltshire SP1 2TJ
tel: +44 (0)1722 410800
fax: +44 (0)1722 410777
email:info@ogarasat.co.uk
Provider of Iridium, Inmarsat and Thuraya services.

Embassies And National Mountaineering Associations

The UK embassies of popular destination for mountain travellers are listed here, along with the mountaineering associations (where available) for expeditions. Email addresses should be treated with suspicion; urgent enquiries are best made in person or by telephone. The majority of embassy web sites contain visa information.

Argentine General Consulate
27 Three Kings Yard
London W1Y 1FL
tel: +44 (0)20 7318 1340
fax: +44 (0)20 7318 1349
e-mail: fclond@mrecic.gov.ar
www.turismo.gov.ar

Bolivian Embassy
106 Eaton Square
London SW1W 9AD
tel: + 44 (0)20 7235 4255
fax: + 44 (0)20 7235 4255

Visit Canada
P.O. Box 5396
Northampton NN1 2FA
tel: 0906 871 5000 (premium rate, recorded info)
email: visitcanada@dial.pipex.com
www.travelcanada.ca

Alpine Club of Canada
P.O. Box 8040 (omit for courier deliveries)
Indian Flats Road
Canmore, AB T1W 2T8
Canada
tel: +1 403 678 3200
fax: +1 403 678 3224
email. alpclub@telusplanet.net
www.alpineclubofcanada.ca

Consulate of Chile
12 Devonshire Street
London W1G 7DS
tel: + 44 (0)20 7580 1023
fax: + 44 (0)20 7323 4294
email: cglonduk@congechileuk.demon.co.uk
www.echileuk.demon.co.uk

Chinese Embassy
31 Portland Place
London W1N 3AG
tel: +44(0)20 7631 1430
tel: 09001 880808 (recorded info)
fax: +44(0)20 7636 9756
www.chinese-embassy.org.uk

Chinese Mountaineering Association
9 Tiyuguan Road
Post Code 100763
Beijing
China
tel: +86 10671 23 796
fax: +86 10 671 11 629
email: cmaex@ina.com.cn

Greenland
Danish Polar Center/Dansk Polarcenter

Strandgade 100H
DK 1401
København K.
Denmark
tel: +45 3288 0100
fax: +45 3288 0101
email: dpc@dpc.dk
www.dpc.dk

Embassy of Ecuador
Flat 3B, 3 Hans Crescent
London SW1X 0LS
tel: +44(0)20 7584 1367
fax: +44(0)20 7823 9701
email: embhadja@ecuador.freeserve.co.uk

High Commission of India
India House
Aldwych
London WC2B 4NA
tel: + 44 (0)20 7836 8484
fax: + 44 (0)20 7836 4331
www.hcilondon.org

Indian Mountaineering Foundation
Benito Juarez Road
New Delhi
110 021
India
tel: +91 11 467 1211
fax: +91 11 688 3412
email: indmount@vsnl.com
www.indmount.com

Embassy of the Republic of Indonesia (for Irian Jaya)
Consular Section, 38a Adams Row
London W1K 2HW
tel: +44 (0)20 7499 7661
fax: +44 (0)20 7491 4993
www.indonesianembassy.org.uk

Consular Section of the Embassy of The Islamic Republic of Iran
50 Kensington Court
London W8 5BB
tel: + 44 (0)20 7937 5225
fax: + 44 (0)20 7938 1615
email: info@iran-embassy.org.uk
www.iran-embassy.org.uk

I. R. Iran Mountaineering Federation
c/o NOC Iran
P.O. Box 15815 -1881,Varzandeh St.,
Mofatteh Ave., Tehran
Islamic Republic of Iran
tel: +98 21 883 9928
fax: +98 21 834 333
email: irmountfed@neda.net

Embassy of Kazakhstan
33 Thurloe Square
London SW7 2SD
tel: + 44 (0)20 7581 4646
fax: + 44 (0)20 7584 9905

Kenyan High Commission
45 Portland Place
London WIN 4AS
tel: +44 (0)20 7636 2371
fax: +44 (0)20 7323 6717

Embassy of the Kyrgyz Republic
Ascot House, 119 Crawford Road
London W1U 6BJ
tel: +44 (0)20 7935 1462
fax: +44 (0)20 7935 7449
email: embassy@kyrgyz-embassy.org.uk
www.kyrgyz-embassy.org.uk

Mongolian Embassy
7 Kensington Court
London W8 5DL
tel: + 44 (0)20 7937 0150
fax: + 44 (0)20 7937 1117

The Embassy of the Kingdom of Morocco
49 Queen's Gate
London SW7 5NE
tel: +44 (0)20 7581 5001
fax: +44 (0)20 7225 3862

Embassy of the Kingdom of Nepal
12a Kensington Palace Gardens
London W8 4QU
tel: +44 (0)20 7229 1594
fax: +44 (0)20 7792 9861
email: info@nepembassy.org.uk
www.nepembassy.org.uk

Nepal Mountaineering Association
P.O. Box 1435
Nag Pokhari, Naxal
Kathmandu
Nepal
tel: +977 1 43 45 25
fax: +977 1 43 45 78
email: office@nma.com.np
www.nma.com.np

New Zealand High Commission
New Zealand House
80 Haymarket
London SW1Y 4TQ
tel: +44 (0)20 7930 8422
fax: +44 (0)20 7839 4580
www.newzealandhc.org.uk

New Zealand Alpine Club
P.O. Box 786
Christchurch
New Zealand
tel: + 64 3 377 75 95
fax: +64 3 377 75 94
email: office@alpineclub.org.nz
www.alpineclub.org.nz

High Commission for Pakistan
36 Lowndes Square
London SW1X 9JN
tel: +44(0)20 7664 9200 (9269)
fax: +44(0)20 7664 9224

Alpine Club of Pakistan
509 Kashmir Road
R.A. Bazar, Rawalpindi
Pakistan
tel: +92 51 927 1321
email: alpineclub@meganet.com.pk
www.pakalpineclub.org.pk

Embassy of Peru
52 Sloane Street
London SW1X 9SP
tel: +44 (0)20 7838 9223
fax: +44 (0)20 7823 2789
email:consulate@peruembassy-uk.com
www.peruembassy-uk.com

Polish Consulate General
73 New Cavendish Street
London W1W 6LS
tel. +44 (0)20 7580 0476
fax +44 (0)20 7323 2320
email: kg.rp.londyn@btclick.com

Embassy of the Russian Federation
5 Kensington Palace Gardens
London W8 4QX
tel: +44 (0)20 7229 8027
fax: +44 (0)20 7229 3215
email: info@rusemblon.org
www.rusemblon.org

South African High Commission
South Africa House
Trafalgar Square
London WC2N 5DP
tel: +44 (0)20 7925 8900
fax: +44 (0)20 7930 1510
email: general@southafricahouse.com
www.southafricahouse.com
Note: consular enquiries are only dealt with by post to
the above address or in person at 15 Whitehall, London
SW1A 2DD.

The Mountain Club of South Africa
97 Hatfield Street
Cape Town 8001
Republic of South Africa
tel: +27 21 465 3412
fax: +27 21 461 8456
email: mcsacc@iafrica.com
www.mcsa.org.za

Tanzania High Commission
43 Hertford Street
London W1Y 8DB
tel: +44 (0)20 7499 8951
fax: +44 (0)20 7491 9321
email: balozi@tanzania-online.gov.uk
www.tanzania-online.gov.uk

Ugandan High Commission
Uganda House
58-59 Trafalgar Square
London WC2N 5DX
tel: +44 (0)20 7839 5783
fax: +44 (0)20 7839 8925

American Embassy
24 Grosvenor Square
London W1A 1AE
tel: +44 (0)20 7499 9000
fax: +44 (0)20 7894 0699
www.usembassy.org.uk

The American Alpine Club
710 Tenth Street
Suite 100
Golden, CO 80401
USA
tel: +1 303 384 0110
fax: +1 303 384 0111
email: getinfo@americanalpineclub.org
www.americanalpineclub.org

British embassies abroad
www.fco.gov.uk/directory/posts.asp

UK Passport Office
tel: 0870 521 0410 (UK only)
www.ukpa.gov.uk
A number of offices exist around the UK for people who
require a passport at such short notice they cannot apply
by post (forms available from post offices).

Libraries That Hold Maps
And Expedition Reports
Alpine Club Library (contact details under advisory
organisations). The AC holds copies of more than 600
expedition reports. The reports may be viewed at the AC
library, and photocopies may be obtained in writing.
There is a charge for this service. The AC Himalayan
Index, a free service which provides basic information
on all known ascents, can be viewed on-line at:
http://himalaya.alpine-club.org.uk.

The library at the **Royal Geographical Society** with the
Institute of British Geographers is closed for renovation
until 2003. The Expedition Advisory Centre (see entry
under 'Advisory Organisations') might be able to assist
with enquiries from non-members.

A number of **British universities** - most notably
Oxford, Cambridge and those with geological
departments - have dedicated libraries that hold maps
not found elsewhere in the UK.

Map And Guidebook Distributors

Chessler Books

P.O. Box 4359

29723 Troutdale Scenic Drive

Evergreen, Colorado 80437

USA

tel: +1 303 670 0093

fax: +1 303 670 9727

email: chesslerbk@aol.com

www.chesslerbooks.com (new books)

www.abebooks.com/home/chesslerbooks (rare books)

Cicerone Press

2 Police Square

Milnthorpe

Cumbria LA7 7PY

tel +44 (0)1539 562 069

fax +44 (0)1539 563 417

email: info@cicerone.co.uk

www.cicerone.co.uk

Cicerone produce around 300 pocket guides to mountain regions in the UK, Europe and other selected destinations worldwide. Cicerone guides are available from retailers or direct from the publisher.

Cordee Ltd

3a De Montfort Street

Leicester LE1 7HD

tel +44 (0)116 254 3579

fax +44 (0)116 247 1176

email: info@cordee.co.uk

www.cordee.co.uk

Cordee, Europe's largest specialist wholesaler of recreation and travel titles, distribute a wide range of climbing and trekking books, maps and videos via the specialist retailer and the book trade, or direct to the public. Visit the website to see what is available.

East View Cartographic Inc.

3020 Harbor Lane North

Minneapolis, MN 55447

USA

tel: 0800 962 388 (toll free from UK) or +1 763 550 0961

fax: 0800 962 707 (toll free from UK) or +1 763 559 2931

email: maps@eastview.com

www.cartographic.com

The most accurate maps available of many countries are produced by the Russian military. East View are able to supply these previously classified maps.

Edward Stanford Ltd

12-14 Long Acre

London WC2E 9LP

tel: +44 (0)20 7836 1321

fax: +44 (0)20 7836 0189

email: sales@stanfords.co.uk

www.stanfords.co.uk

Omni Resources

1004 South Mebane Street

PO Box 2096

Burlington, NC 27216-2096

USA

Tel: +1 336 227 8300

Fax: +1 336 227 3748

www.omnimap.com

custserve@omnimap.com

Omni hold a large stock of Russian military, FBI and CIA maps that often provide the only cartographical coverage of more remote destinations.

The Map Shop

15 High Street

Upton upon Severn

Worcestershire WR8 0HJ

tel: +44 (0)1684 593146

fax: +44 (0)1684 594559

email: themapshop@btinternet.com

www.themapshop.co.uk

The **BMC Information Service** has its own bookstore (contact details can be found under 'Advisory Organisations').

Suppliers Of Secondhand Books

You may find that many recommended books and guides are out-of-print. If so, the following companies might be able to assist.

Advanced Book Exchange

abebooks.com

The world's largest network of independent booksellers.

Cheyne Books For Mountaineers

8 Cheyne Road

Prudhoe

Northumberland NE42 6PE

tel: +44 (0)1661 833897

email: dek@cheynebooks.demon.co.uk

Jarvis Books
57 Smedley Street East
Matlock
Derbyshire DE4 3FQ
tel/fax: +44 (0)1629 55322
email: jarvis@mountainbooks.co.uk
www.mountainbooks.co.uk

Equipment Repairers
Feet First Direct Ltd
Units 4/5
Foundry Industrial Estate
Whittington Moor
Chesterfield S41 9AU
tel: +44 (0)1246 260795
email: info@resoles.co.uk
www.feetfirst.resoles.co.uk

Mountaineering Designs
PO Box 20
Grange-over-Sands
Cumbria LA11 6GD
tel: +44 (0)15395 36333
email: enquiries@mountaineering-designs.co.uk
www.mountaineering-designs.co.uk
Offers a refurbishment service for down sleeping bags

Shoecare
Rothwell St
Bolton BL3 6HY
tel: 0800 028 6876 (toll free in UK) or +44 (0)1204 525566
fax +44 (0)1204 364265
email: repairs@shoecare-eu.com
www.shoecare-eu.com
A repair service for most types of outdoor clothing,
equipment and footwear.

Tent Repair Service
The Old Stables
Station Road
Musselburgh EH21 7PF
Scotland
tel: +44 (0)131 653 6114
fax: +44 (0)131 665 0129
email: info@tentrepair.com
www.tentrepair.com

W. E. Franklin
116 - 120 Onslow Rd
Sheffield S11 7AH

tel: +44 (0)114 268 6161
email: info@franklinsgroup.co.uk
www.franklinsgroup.co.uk
Offers a wet cleaning service for down products.

Children
Outdoor Kids
The Minories
Stratford upon Avon CV37 6NF
Phone: +44 (0)1789 414791
Fax: +44 (0)1789 414781
email: info@outdoorkids.co.uk
www.outdoorkids.co.uk

Organisations Concerned With Local People And The Mountain Environment
International Porter Protection Group
email: info@ippg.net
www.ippg.net

International Year of Mountains
www.mountains2002.org

Mountain Forum
www2.mtnforum.org

The Mountain Institute
www.mountain.org

Tourism Concern
Stapleton House
277-281 Holloway Road
London N7 8HN
tel: +44 (0)20 7753 3330
fax: +44 (0)20 7753 3331
email: info@tourismconcern.org.uk
www.tourismconcern.org.uk

UK Himalayan Trust
Lowecroft, Plains Lane
Blackbrook, Belper
Derby DE56 2DD
tel/fax: +44 (0)1773 823831
email: georgeandmary@lowecroft.freeserve.co.uk
Raises funds to support Sir Edmund Hillary's Himalayan
Trust. Westerners are rarely invited to become involved
directly with ventures as local people are employed by
the Trust to carry out the work, but the Trust welcomes
supporters who wish to raise funds.

Organisations That Cater For Disabled People

Adventure Designs

Design for Life Centre
Brunel University
Runneymede
Surrey TW20 0JZ
tel: +44 (0)1784 433262
fax: +44 (0)1784 470880
email: adventure-designs-dfl@brunel.ac.uk
www.brunel.ac.uk/research/dfl/dflad.htm
The primary focus of this team's work is equipment design. Their range of products include a climbing harness. The Expedition Advisory Centre (EAC) and the Design for Life Centre have formed a partnership to provide advice, information and support to disabled explorers and those organising inclusive expeditions involving disabled and able-bodied members. (Contact details under EAC entry in 'Advisory Organisations'.)

High Hopes Adventures

4 Grange Close
Leybourne
West Malling
Kent ME19 5HU
tel/fax: +44 (0)1732 848785
email: high-hopes-adventures@care4free.net
www.high-hopes-adventures.care4free.net

National Ability Center

PO Box 682799
Park City, Utah
84068-2799
USA
tel: +1 435 649 3991
fax: +1 435 658 3992
nac@xmission.com
www.nationalabilitycenter.org
Offers a range of outdoor activities including alpine sports, hiking and camping.

National Sports Center For The Disabled

PO Box 1290, Winter Park
Colorado 80482
USA
tel: +1 970 726 1540/+1 303 316 1540
fax: +1 970 726 4112
email: info@nscd.org
www.nscd.org

SportABILI Onlus

Via dei Lagorai
113 - 38037 Predazzo (TN)
Italy
tel: +39 (0)462 501999
fax: +39 (0)462 507707
email: info@sportabili.org
www.sportabili.org

Uphill Ski Club

6a Emson Close
Saffron Walden
Essex CB10 1HL
tel/fax: +44 (0)1799 525406
email: enquiries@uphill-ski-club.demon.co.uk
www.uphillskiclub.co.uk

Guides

British Mountain Guides (BMG)

Capel Curig
Gwynedd
Wales LL24 0ET
tel: +44 (0)1690 720 386
fax: +44 (0)1690 720 248
email: bmg@mltb.org
www.bmg.org.uk

Grants

Mount Everest Foundation (MEF)

W.H. Ruthven
Gowrie
Cardwell Close
Warton
Preston PR4 1SH
tel/fax: +44 (0)1772 635346
email: bill.ruthven@ukgateway.net
www.alpine-club.org.uk/mef/mef.htm
www.mef.org.uk
The MEF awards grants to British and New Zealand expeditions planning mountaineering exploration or research in high mountain regions. The MEF also awards the Alison Chadwick Memorial Grant, 'To further British and Polish women's mountaineering in the Greater Ranges'.

Details of other exploratory, climbing and ski-mountaineering grants for individuals and expeditions can be found at:
www.bmc.co.uk/mountaintravel.htm

Appendix B: Expedition Planning Timetable

There are so many things to consider when planning your first expedition to a mountain environment that you might find these monthly 'to do' lists to be of some use. Expeditions that have less time than the ideal, or who are departing at different times of the year to the example outlined here, will want to adjust their timetable accordingly. All expeditions are unique, and so some of the issues raised here are likely to prove inappropriate to your venture. For example, if all the members of the team are known to you, it is unlikely that a formal selection process will need to be instigated. Similarly, if you do not intend to chase sponsorship or grants, then some of the fundraising points will prove somewhat irrelevant.

PRE-EXPEDITION PHASE

October/November
- Research the objective
- Organise a weekend away for prospective members
- Choose team members
- Start applying for any climbing or trekking permits
- Draft budget (update regularly thereafter)
- Design headed paper and expedition brochure or leaflet
- Investigate and begin applying for appropriate grants
- Consider attending the EAC expedition planning seminar
- Book any specialist training courses (e.g. medical)
- Carry out risk assessment (update regularly thereafter)
- Draw up personal and group equipment lists
- Open bank account
- Make contact with in-country agent

December/January
- Finalise team
- Obtain a financial commitment from everyone
- Delegate tasks
- Carry out reconnaissance visit to region if appropriate
- Initiate fundraising events
- Contact potential sponsors and supporters
- Write and distribute first press release to media
- Draw up environmental policy

February/March
- Make follow-up calls to potential sponsors & supporters
- Secure purchasing arrangements for bulk orders of equipment with outdoor retailers
- Procure necessary medical supplies

- Begin vaccination and blood grouping programme
- Contact publications with proposals for articles
- Insure expedition members and local staff (the latter is normally done through in-country agents)

April/May
- Send second press release to media
- Make hard copies of all relevant paperwork
- Finalise budget
- Contact home embassy in host country
- Handover to home country expedition contact person
- Send any freight early enough to arrive in-country before expedition departs
- Ensure team, hosts and UK contact are aware of emergency procedures

EXPEDITION PHASE

June/July
- Liaise with in-country agents
- Establish communication link with home
- Retrieve equipment from customs
- Make a final check of equipment in-country before departing for Base Camp
- Call or write to expedition sponsors and supporters
- Maintain detailed notes of expenditure
- Keep diaries for purposes of expedition report and any articles
- Ensure that environmental procedures are followed

POST-EXPEDITION PHASE

August/September
- Send letters of thanks to in-country hosts
- Write preliminary report for grant-giving organisations
- Send letters of thanks and photos to sponsors
- Complete expedition accounts

October onwards
- Produce expedition report and distribute
- Honour promises to sponsors and supporters
- Deliver expedition lecture
- Write articles
- Begin researching next expedition...

Appendix C: Equipment Checklists

Suggested kit lists for popular destinations are described below. They are meant as a guide only: for example, people who know they feel the cold may want to include additional items of clothing. Mountaineers attempting more ambitious routes than those described here will require additional climbing hardware.

The five kit lists follow a modular design, with each list building on the previous one(s). It is possible to build your collection of clothing and equipment over a period of time as your experience increases, without having to upgrade too many items. If your long-term goal is attempting routes on high mountains then investing in, for example, waterproof/breathable trousers with full-length zips early on in your mountaineering career will save you money in the long term.

For a trek along the Inca Trail to Machu Picchu with a commercial operator:
T-shirt
Underwear
Wicking base layer
Wind-resistant trousers
Fleece jacket
Waterproof/breathable jacket and trousers
Sun hat
Warm hat
Gloves
Leather or fabric boots
Walking socks
Iodine tablets or liquid
Two water bottles
Sleeping bag rated to -5˚C
Sleeping bag liner
Closed-cell foam or open-cell self-inflating mattress
Daysack for personal things
Holdall for porter load
Trekking poles
Repair kit (see next page)
First aid kit inc. personal medication
Sunblock, lipsalve, footpowder
100% UV sunglasses
Torch & spare batteries
Camera, film, batteries

Personal insurance, passport, money, visa and permit
Guidebook (with sketch map) and phrase book
Whistle
Penknife (with scissors)
Wash kit

For an independent tea house trek in Nepal to Everest Base Camp during the pre-monsoon or post-monsoon season. As for Inca Trail plus:
Lightweight duvet (approx. 150-200g down)
Fleece trousers
60-70 litre rucksack
Map
Sleeping bag rated to -10˚C (or upgrade Machu Picchu sleeping bag with fleece liner)
Inexpensive, lightweight, waterproof/breathable sleeping bag cover (in case of failure to reach tea house)
Note: little need for waterproof-breathable trousers

These first two kit lists serve well as guides for treks in many mountain regions, from Patagonia to the Pamirs. The climate of the region, the time of year, the difficulty of the terrain and the level of remoteness will determine any changes to the warmth of the sleeping bag, level of water resistance of your outer layers, provision of a compass etc. Additional requirements for three other popular objectives are given below.

For an ascent of Kilimanjaro with a commercial operator. As for Everest Base Camp plus:
Extra base layer
Gaiters
Umbrella
Insect repellent
Daysack and holdall from Machu Picchu list; no need for a large rucksack
Long johns (wear with fleece trousers on summit day if necessary)
Fleece-lined waterproof/breathable mittens
Box-wall duvet jacket (approx. 300g down)
Sleeping bag rated to -15˚C (or upgrade sleeping bag for Everest Base Camp sleeping bag with fleece liner)

For an independent ascent of a 6000m
peak in the Himalaya or Karakoram.
As for Kilimanjaro, plus:

Plastic boots

Crampons (and adjusting tools)

Ice axe

Climbing equipment (inc. ice hammer if the terrain
justifies its use)

Mountain tent

Stove & fuel bottle

Board to prevent stove tilting into snow

Cooking kit

Compass

Altimeter

Plastic insulated mug and lid

Goggles

Bivouac bag

Waterproof/breathable trousers or salopettes with
full-length side zips

For an independent ascent of Mount
McKinley (Denali) via the West Buttress.
As for 6000m peak, plus:

Neoprene face mask

Vapour barrier socks

Vapour barrier sleeping bag liner

Pee bottle

Insulated booties

Insulated salopettes (depending on the season)

Neoprene overboots

Skis and skins or snowshoes

Toboggan for transporting loads on glacier (usually
provided by air taxi service)

Down-filled or open cell foam mittens

Grain shovel (bought in Anchorage; larger blade than UK
snow shovels)

Snow saw

Additional fuel containers ('White Gas' fuel usually
provided by air taxi service)

Second sleeping mat

Sleeping bag rated to -30°C

Replace fleece trousers with pile salopettes

Note: umbrella, insect repellent and leather/fabric boots
from previous kit lists not required

Repair kit

It is always a good idea to take along a repair kit in case
a strap breaks, a tent flysheet tears or a self-inflating
mattress deflates. The contents of your kit will depend
on what gear you might need to service, and where you
are going. Remember that files and spanners that are
taken along to adjust your ice tools and crampons can be
pressed into service as repair tools. A pocket multitool
with built-in pliers and screwdrivers is also useful for
effecting running repairs.

A basic repair kit might include:

A tough polythene screw-top beaker, to hold the
contents of the kit and protect it from being crushed.
Roll several metres of duct tape around the beaker – this
can be peeled off when required. A tube of
cyanoacrylate glue (i.e. 'Superglue') for fixing solid but
slightly flexible items such as sunglasses, earphones and
credit cards: this glue is also useful for holding things
together whilst splinting or binding. Small folding
scissors; small roll of thin, narrow sticky tape; a biro and
a sheet of paper; a metal tube for fixing a broken tent
pole (hold in position with gaffer tape); prickers and
spares for your stove; length of 1.5mm perlon cord; a
vulcanising rubber solution and rubber repair sheet for
self-inflating mattress and similar repairs; assorted
needles; plenty of polyester thread.

A more extensive repair kit might also
contain:

A small tube of thixotropic impact adhesive (for gluing
fabrics and other flexible bonds such as leather and most
rubbers) gives you a little time when joining two
things together: it also works when a laminate needs to
be formed, such as when patching. A two-part mini
epoxy glue, for fixing similar heavier items such as ski
pole tips. A thimble; 15cm of Velcro; a few hand-sized
pieces of fleece, ripstop nylon and waterproof nylon; a
reel of Kevlar fishing gut for sewing rucksacks etc.; a
piece of tightly-folded emery cloth for roughing up and
sharpening; a small, strong, metal snap-blade utility knife
with spare blades; 0.5m of thin plastic coated wire for
electrical repairs or binding; 0.5m of iron wire for
binding; mini screwdriver for glasses and shades.

Appendix D: Medical Kits

The following modular packs are designed for one adult. Two people travelling together are advised to increase most quantities by 50%. Three people are advised to increase most quantities by 75%.

Pack 1: Recommended first aid kit to take to all countries

Item	Description	Quantity
Sticking plaster (e.g. Bandaid)	For minor cuts	assorted
Triangular bandage	Variety of uses including slings and immobilising limbs: an item of clothing can also be used as an improvised triangular bandage	1
Latex examination gloves	To protect victim and first aider	1 pair
Tweezers	For removing thorns etc. (some penknives have tweezers)	1
Scissors	For cutting dressings. Some scissors are also designed to cut clothing	1
Micropore	For securing dressings	1 roll
'Release' dressing	Non-adherent dressing for wounds	1
'Bactigras' dressing	10cm x 10cm For minor burns	3
Lightweight bandages	For holding wound dressings in place	1
Support bandage	For supporting sprains	1
Sterile gauze swab	7.5cm x 7.5cm, for cleaning wounds and padding	2 packs of 5
Steristrips	Temporary closures for large wounds	1 pack
Cling film	For covering larger burns during transportation to hospital	small roll
thermometer	Either forehead or digital type	1
Betadine dry powder spray	For disinfecting skin, wounds and burns	1 spray (150g)

Pack 2: Recommended drugs to take to all countries

Drug	Description	Details	Quantity	Dose
Clarithromycin	Respiratory infection, skin infection, animal bites and toothache	500mg tablets	14	500mg every 12 hours for 7 days.
Ciprofloxacin	Traveller's diarrhoea, urinary tract infections and respiratory tract infections.	500mg tablets	14	500mg every 12 hours for 7 days.
Metronidazole	Toothache, also for cases of traveller's diarrhoea that do not improve after 1 week of Ciprofloxacin (no alcohol during or 48 hours after course)	400mg tablets	21	400mg every 8 hours for 7 days.
Buccastem	Nausea and vomiting	3mg tablets	10	3mg once or twice daily taken under the tongue until it has dissolved (do not swallow).

Drug	Description	Details	Quantity	Dose
Loperamide	Severe diarrhoea	2mg capsules	24	4mg initially, followed by 2mg after each loose stool for up to 5 days. Max. 16mg daily
Paracetamol	Fever, pain	500mg tablets	20	1000mg every 6hrs. Max. 8 tablets in 24 hours.
Ibuprofen	Pain (sprains, aches etc.): contra-indicated in asthmatics	200mg tablets	30	400mg every 8 hours after food.
Diclofenac	For pain and fever, if unable to take tablets orally: contra-indicated in asthmatics	100mg rectal suppositories	2	100mg every 12 hours.

Pack 3: Recommended drugs to take to treat altitude sickness

Drug	Description	Details	Quantity	Dose
Acetazolamide	Treatment of AMS (for preventative regime see Chapter 10)	250mg tablets	12	250mg every 8 hours for 2 days.
Nifedipine	For High Altitude Pulmonary Oedema (HAPE)	20mg tablets	5	20mg immediately, then 20mg after 6, 12, 18hrs (max 80mg).
Dexamethasone	For High Altitude Cerebral Oedema (HACE)	2mg tablets	12	8mg immediately, then 4mg after 6, 12, 18 hrs (max 20mg).
Amethocaine	Local anaesthetic eye drops for snowblindness (emergencies only)	one-use container (minims)	2	Two drops in each affected eye for pain control as and when required.

Pack 4: Sterile kit for countries without first class medical facilities

Item	Description/details	Quantity
Syringe	5ml	3
Hypodermic needles	Green	5
Infusion set	Blood giving	1
Intravenous cannulae ('drip')	18 gauge and 14 gauge	1 of each
Nylon suture	3/0; straight needle	1

Pack 5: Optional items (depending on personal health and destination)

Item	Description	Details	Quantity	Dose
Chloramphenicol	Eye ointment	n/a	1 tube	Apply a smear to the inside of the lower eyelid 4 times a day.
Sofradex	Ear drops	n/a	10ml bottle	Apply 2 drops 3 times a day to the ear.
Fluconazole	Vaginal thrush	150mg tablets	2	1 tablet.
Water purification tablets or droplets	Iodine or chlorine, for treating contaminated water	n/a	50	As per supplied instructions: dosage may need to be increased in heavily contaminated or cold water.
Loratadine	Symptomatic relief of allergy (and limited insect bite relief)	10mg tablets	10	10 mg once daily.
Eurax cream	For treating itchy bites	30g tube	1	n/a
Canesten HC	For treating fungal infections	20g tube	1	n/a
Bactroban ointment	Antibiotic for infected cuts	15g tube (2%)	1	n/a
Ranitidine tablets	Antacid for stomach ulcers and/or gastritis	150mg tablets	8	300mg at night.
Cyclizine	For motion sickness (may cause drowsiness and affect performance of skilled tasks. Effects of alcohol enhanced).	50mg tablets	As required	50mg every 8 hours. First dose 1 hour before journey.
Tampons & condoms	n/a	n/a	As required	n/a
Insect repellent	Quantity and strength depends on the area to be visited. 'Mosiguard' recommended by London School of Tropical Medicine. Apply to exposed skin. Note that some insects bite during the day, whilst others bite at night.	n/a	As required	
Malarial prophylaxis	For the prevention of malaria: seek professional advice before departure as to appropriate regime. It is recommended that malaria prophylactic tablets are started before departure and continued after leaving the malarial zone as advised.	n/a	As advised	As advised
Quinine	Treatment of Falciparum malaria (the type that causes fatal cerebral malaria). Seek expert medical advice and consider urgent repatriation.	600mg tablets	21	600mg every 8 hours for 7 days.
Doxycycline	A course of Doxycycline will be started after completing a course of Quinine for the treatment of Falciparum malaria in areas known to have Quinine resistance. Seek expert medical advice and consider urgent repatriation.	100mg	14	After completing Quinine course, start Doxycycline 100mg every 12 hrs for 7 days.

General notes

1. The content of this appendix is a suggestion only, and is in no way a substitute for up-to-date professional medical advice.
2. GPs have current treatment guidelines. You should therefore seek the advice of your local doctor before travelling.
3. Self diagnosis is to be heavily discouraged, even when the patient is a qualified doctor. This applies to every medical condition.
4. Precise clinical diagnosis without modern laboratory facilities can be very difficult, even for highly skilled medical doctors.
5. Many different diseases can mimic each other with their symptoms.

Notes for all medications

1. These drugs are for ADULTS only.
2. Whenever possible, obtain the advice of an adequately trained healthcare professional before using any medication. (Your assistance company might be able to arrange for a doctor to speak to you.)
3. Always read the literature which comes with the medicines. Note indications, contra-indications, recommended doses and any side-effects.
4. Do not exceed recommended doses.
5. Are you allergic to any components of the medicine?
6. Store medicines as directed.
7. Do not use out-of-date medicines (check the stamp on container).
8. If you are already taking medication (including over-the-counter or herbal products) beware of possible drug interactions.
9. Women who are pregnant, or likely to become pregnant, should seek professional medical advice before taking ANY drug.
10. Always carry the appropriate prescriptions.

Notes for medical equipment

1. Wherever possible, all medical equipment (including needles, stitching material and drips) should be handled by people who have received training in their correct use.
2. Do not share needles or stitching materials.
3. Always read any supplied instructions.

Appendix E: Bibliography

Books are listed under specific categories with title, author/editor, publisher and international standard book number (ISBN) details where available. Some books may be out-of-print; a list of suppliers of secondhand book suppliers is included in Appendix A, alongside book distributors of current titles. Telephone numbers are included next to particularly hard-to-obtain books.

Medical

Altitude Illness Prevention, Recognition & Treatment. Bezruchka. Cordee. 1871890578

Bugs, Bites and Bowels. Wilson-Howarth. Cadogan Guides. 186011914x

Expedition Medicine For Doctors And Non-Medics. Eds: Warrell & Anderson. 1861970404

First Aid And Survival In Mountain And Remote Areas (7th Ed.). Duff & Gorm. Treksafe. 0646417827

Medicine For Mountaineering. Wilkerson. The Mountaineers Books. 0898867991

Red Cross First Aid Manual. Red Cross. 0751307076

Sporting Injuries, A Self-Help Guide. Grisogono. John Murray. 0719541115

The High Altitude Medicine Handbook. Pollard & Murdoch. Radcliffe Medical Press. 1857752147

Traveller's Health. Dawood. Oxford University Press. 0192622471

Your Child's Health Abroad. Howarth & Ellis. Bradt Publications. 1898323631

Backpacking and Trekking

Safety on Mountains. BMC. 0903908271

Beyond Backpacking, Jardine Adventure Lore Press. 0963235931

Snow Sense. Fredston. Alaska Mountain Safety Centre. 0964399407

The Advanced Backpacker. Townsend. Ragged Mountain Press. 0071357564

The Backpacker's Handbook. Townsend. Ragged Mountain Press. 0070653151

Climbing and Expeditions

Alpine Climbing. Barry. The Crowood Press. 1852238887

Avalanche Safety For Skiers & Climbers. Daffern. Baton Wicks. 1898573441

Expedition Planners' Handbook. Eds: Winser & McWilliam. Expedition Advisory Centre. 0907649548. (This book is the primary source of information on all aspects of planning an expedition, from inception to the final report. A new edition of the Expedition Handbook is currently being prepared. Copies of individual chapters are available on request from the Expedition Advisory Centre: contact details in Appendix A.)

Exploring New Frontiers. Edwards. Royal Scottish Geographical Society. (To order, call +44 (0)141 552 3330)

Extreme Alpinism. Twight. The Mountaineers Books. 089886654

Glacier Travel & Crevasse Rescue. Summers. Diadem. 0906371589

Handbook Of Climbing. Fyffe & Peters. Penguin. 0720720540

Joining An Expedition. Ed: Winser. Expedition Advisory Centre. 0907649734

Lightweight Expeditions. Collister. The Crowood Press. 1852231394

Mountaineering: The Freedom Of The Hills. Ed: Graydon & Hanson, Airlife Publishing 1840370017

The Complete Manual Of Modern Rope Techniques. Shepherd. Constable. 1841193232

The Mountain Skills Training Handbook. Hill & Johnston. 0715310917

Note: Cordee are the book distributors for the Alpine Journal, the American Alpine Journal and the Himalayan Journal. (Cordee's contact details can be found in Appendix A).

Environmental

Environmental Responsibility For Expeditions. Eds: Workman, Gimingham & Jermy. Young Explorers' Trust/British Ecological Society. 1900579006

How To Shit In The Woods. Meyer. 10-Speed Press. 0898153190

Leave No Trace. McGiveney. The Mountaineers Books. 0898865247

Culture and Community Tourism

Community-Based Mountain Tourism: Practices For linking Conservation With Enterprise. Ed: Godde. (To order, visit http://www.mtnforum.org/resources/orders/publications.htm)

Mountains of the World: Tourism and Sustainable Mountain Development. Eds: Price, Wachs & Byers. Mountain Agenda. (To order, call +44 (0)20 7753 3330)

The Community Tourism Guide. Mann. Tourism Concern/Earthscan. 1853836818

The Culture Shock! series of guidebooks give specific country advice on cultural matters. For details of countries covered write to: Kupernard, 311 Ballards Lane, London N12 8LY, or email: mail@kuperard.co.uk. www.cultureshockguides.com

Parents, Children and Young People

Are We Nearly There? Samantha Gore Lyons. Virgin Books. 0753503999

Have Baby Will Travel. Lennard Publishing. 1852911433

Mountains. Moonlight Publishing. 1851032940. (for children aged approx. 3-6)

Mountains of the World. Moonlight Publishing. 1851030654 (for children aged approx. 7-12)

Parents' Guide to Hiking & Camping. A Trailside Guide. Cary. WW Norton. 0393316521

Safe And Responsible Youth Expeditions And Code Of Practice For Youth Expeditions. Putnam. Young Explorers' Trust. 0905965043

Travel With Children. Wheeler. Lonely Planet. 0864422997

Navigation

Art of Outdoor Navigation. Hurn. (CD-ROM)

GPS Made Easy. Letham. Rocky Mountain Books. 0921102666

Mountain Navigation. Cliffe. Peter Cliffe. 1871890551

Navigation For Walkers. Tippett. Cordee. 1871890543

BMC Publications

Knots; Ropes; Crampons; Alpine Skills; Winter Skills; East Africa; India; Nepal; Pakistan; South America. (For details of all these publications contact the BMC: contact details in Appendix A.)

Other

Conditioning For Outdoor Fitness. Musnick. The Mountaineers Books. 089886450x

Outdoor Leadership Handbook. Graham. The Mountaineers Books. 0898865026

Survival Of The Fittest. Stroud. Random House. 0099272598

The Traveller's Handbook. Eds: Lorie & Sohanpaul. Footprint Handbooks. 090580211x

Travel Photography. L'Anson. Lonely Planet. 186450207X

Weather Handbook. Watts. Thomas Reed Publications. 1840370890

Women Travel. Rough Guides. Rough Guides.1858284597

Appendix F: The Work Of The BMC

The British Mountaineering Council (BMC) promotes the interests of climbers, hill walkers and mountaineers in Britain, and supports its members when they travel abroad. The work of the BMC falls into two broad categories; development projects and members services.

Development Projects
Access and Conservation
Two full-time officers are committed to increasing and maintaining access to mountains and crags, and work closely with landowners and conservation bodies to resolve any practical difficulties. The officers are supported by a network of voluntary Access Representatives. This team is augmented with specialists who assist with complex legal, scientific and development issues.

The BMC is deeply involved in lobbying the government to increase open access to the countryside: the BMC's action helped to ensure that the Countryside Rights of Way (CROW) act was passed in Parliament, establishing a right of access to open country, defined as mountain and moorland. (At the time of writing, the bill is not yet in complete effect as these areas of open country must be mapped.) The BMC's approach of diplomatic negotiation to secure and retain access to crags that are not covered by the CROW act has been successful in many areas. However, despite continuing efforts, many important walking and climbing areas remain off-limits for reasons which the BMC believes are unjustified.

The officers also work closely with conservation agencies to resolve any potential conflict. The BMC publishes information on sites where climbing restrictions are necessary to protect endangered bird species and rare flora: these restrictions are reviewed on a regular basis. Good practice guidelines are also published for groups and individuals. These give advice on measures to reduce erosion at crags and protect the environment. Furthermore, the BMC is a founder member of the British Upland Footpath Trust, which aims to promote quality, non-intrusive upland footpath repair work and management; the BMC provides staff and funding in support of the Trust. Many inappropriate developments threaten the character of Britain's uplands. In partnership with other mountaineering and countryside organisations the BMC engages in campaigns against proposals such as the Cairngorms' funicular railway and the testing of military weapons in National Parks. The BMC also plays a role in the development of policy that affects climbers and walkers: rural transport initiatives are just one issue which the BMC is currently involved in. The BMC's Access Fund is a vital tool in raising funds for the Access and Conservation programme. Trade partners give valuable support, whilst donations from BMC members make a substantial contribution to the projects that are undertaken. At the start of 2002, 'The Access and Conservation Trust' will be launched. Jointly run by a number of organisations including the BMC, the Mountaineering Council of Scotland (MCofS) and mountain training boards, this charity will co-ordinate and support regional access and conservation programmes throughout the UK.

Climbing Walls
With the growing popularity of indoor walls, the BMC is regularly called upon for advice and information from climbers, developers and wall managers. Information from climbing wall experts is contained within the BMC Climbing Wall Manual. For people who want to find their nearest wall, the BMC Climbing Wall Directory is an essential tool.

Youth
The BMC sees its youth program as one of its most important areas of work. Since 1997 the young climbers membership section, 'Gripped?', has existed (complete with its own magazine). The British Regional Youth Competition Series is popular and widely supported; the annual final is one of the best-attended rock climbing competition events. The youth program also includes a series of festivals, outdoor meets and 'Next Step' events.

Competitions

The BMC organises the annual British Indoor Climbing Championship as well World Cup events that are held in the UK. Senior and junior teams are selected and sent to foreign events together with a team manager.

Training

The BMC's primary function is to co-ordinate informal training opportunities and educational material. Key programs include nationwide lectures on winter mountaineering and summer alpine climbing and an annual seminar for students. The BMC also administer the Jonathan Conville Memorial Trust which runs subsidised training courses for young people under the tutelage of British Mountain Guides. A number of videos and books complement the training programmes. In 1996 the BMC, the Mountain Leader Training Board (MLTB) and the United Kingdom Mountain Training Board (UKMTB) formed the Mountain Training Trust (MTT) which took over the running of Plas y Brenin, the National Mountain Centre, situated in the heart of the Snowdonia National Park. The BMC works closely with the MTT.

International

The BMC administers UK Sports Council Grants to British expeditions. Every year, tens of thousands of pounds are awarded to British expeditions. In many cases it is this grant money that makes the expedition financially viable. Other activities in this area include the organisation of the annual BMC International Meet and the production of guidelines on subjects such as culture, the environment and the employment of local staff on expeditions.

Technical

The BMC carries out investigations into failed equipment and oversees corrective measures where necessary. BMC representatives helped to draft European standards for equipment and these appear to have reduced the number of equipment failures. Advice and information are also an important part of the BMC's technical work and much of this knowledge is disseminated via a series of booklets.

Heritage

The BMC supports the preservation and display of Mountain Heritage material, of which Britain has a fine supply. In 2000 the BMC launched the Mountain Heritage Trust to develop the Heritage Initiative. In the summer of 2001 the National Exhibition of Mountaineering opened in Cumbria.

Member Services

Membership is open to all climbers and trekkers of any age and ability. Benefits include:

- Access to mountaineering and adventure travel insurance policies
- Personal and liability insurance
- Discounts on publications, videos and magazines (including 'High Mountain Sports')
- A subscription to the quarterly magazine, 'Summit'
- Access to the Information Service, a one-stop shop for outdoor information and advice. Summary sheets covering over 130 countries, and detailed advice packs for new members – as well as subjects such as winter and alpine skills – are also available.

Membership and insurance is available online at www.thebmc.co.uk or over the 'phone on +44 (0)161 445 4747. *Full contact details for the BMC can be found in Appendix A.*

Contributors' Biographies

The youngest member of the first successful Everest Expedition, **George Band** made the first ascent of Kanchenjunga with Joe Brown in 1955. In recent years, George has visited Bhutan, Sikkim, Nepal, Tibet and the Nanda Devi Sanctuary. A former President of the Alpine Club and the British Mountaineering Council, George is currently the Chairman of the Alpine Club Library and a Trustee of the UK branch of Sir Edmund Hillary's Himalayan Trust.

A former Royal Marine and Director of the National Centre for Mountain Activities, **John Barry** is the author of several books including *The Great Climbing Adventure*.

A former officer with the Royal Marines and British Antarctic Survey, British Mountain Guide **Steve Bell** now runs an expedition company. He was the first Briton to guide clients to the summit of an 8000m peak.

Ed de la Billière first travelled to Alaska to assist disabled climber Reggie Perrin in his quest to climb Denali. Ed subsequently returned to Alaska and competed in the 'Iditarod'; a 1200-mile dog sled race.

Chris Bonington has led or joined 20 Himalayan expeditions. He has made dozens of first ascents around the world. The author of 15 books, Chris has been President of the Alpine Club and the British Mountaineering Council, and is currently Chairman of the Mountain Heritage Trust.

Dr Charles Clarke has been climbing in the Himalaya since the 1960s. A doctor on two Everest expeditions, he has recently been exploring Tibet. He runs the UIAA's Mountain Medical Data Centre, which is housed at the BMC.

A professional mountain photographer for 40 years, **John Cleare** was a member of the 1971 International Everest Expedition and has climbed extensively worldwide. He has made several television broadcasts and films including *The Eiger Sanction*. He runs his own picture library.

Phil Coates is a producer and production consultant with extensive experience of filming in remote regions for the BBC and ITV broadcasters. He has led expeditions to South America, the Himalaya and Central Asia, and attempted two 8000ers: Broad Peak and Makalu.

John Cousins is a British Mountain Guide, an advisor on leader training to the Union Internationale des Associations d'Alpinisme and the Executive Secretary to the United Kingdom Mountain Training Board.

A freelance writer, lecturer and award-winning filmmaker, **Jim Curran** has climbed and filmed on 10 Himalayan expeditions, as well as in the Andes, Caucasus, Atlas and China. He is the author of several books.

Smiler Cuthbertson is a British Mountain Guide. He runs Scottish winter and summer alpine courses, and leads expeditions to the Himalaya, East Africa and the Andes.

A keen mountaineer, **Karen Darke** was paralysed from the chest down in a climbing accident at the age of 21. Since then, Karen's focus has shifted to wheelchair racing, skiing and sea kayaking. Her hand-cycling journeys have included a traverse of the Karakoram from Kazakhstan to Pakistan.

The first Australian woman to climb Cho Oyu, **Sue Fear** has climbed and trekked in the Himalaya, Pamirs, Andes, Tien Shan, Karakoram and Southern Alps. Sue runs trips for a leading adventure travel company.

Between 1995 and 2000, **Nick Foxton** spent the best part of a year tracking wildlife in some of the most isolated corners of Tibet, often alone and in the dead of winter.

Since climbing Mont Blanc in 1978 at the age of 17, **Jerry Gore** has managed to wangle an expedition abroad every year. His fascination with climbing has involved him in all the disciplines including big wall and the 8000m game.

A chartered physiotherapist specialising in sports injuries, **Vivian Grisogono** is a former British team physio at summer and winter Olympics, and the author of several books.

Caroline Hamilton was the leader of the first all-women expedition to the North Pole, and leader of the first British women expedition to the South Pole. She is the author of *To The Pole*.

David Hamilton (no relation) has been leading mountaineering, trekking and ski-touring expeditions to the Karakoram for 15 years. His summit successes include Gasherbrum I and II, Tirich Mir and Spantik.

Martin Hartley has been the photographer on the Motorola Pamirs Expedition, the Sheer 7 Borneo Expedition and the Shackleton Memorial Expedition. Martin specialises in medium-format adventure photography.

Peter Hillary began climbing at the age of 10 when he roped up with his father, Sir Edmund. Peter has led or joined expeditions to many of the world's highest mountains including Everest, K2, Makalu and Lhotse. He runs his own adventure travel company.

Dr David Hillebrandt has travelled through over 30 countries and joined expeditions in the Himalaya, Mongolia and Patagonia. A medical advisor to the BMC, David has published a research paper on the medical educational needs of British Mountain Guides.

Since 1988, **Stephen Jones** has been on 20 expeditions to the Arctic, Alaska, Canada, the Karakoram and the Caucasus. In 1993 he led the youngest team to cross the Greenland icecap. Since 1995 he has worked as a professional expedition leader for Raleigh International.

Harish Kapadia has spent four decades exploring the Himalaya. 21 of the 33 peaks he has climbed have been first ascents. He is the editor of the *Himalayan Journal*.

Nick Lewis is a director of an environmental and logistical consulting group. He has climbed in the Polish Tatras, Alaska, Yukon, Yosemite, Tien Shan, Andes and Patagonia.

For more than 20 years, **Tim Macartney-Snape** has climbed and trekked through the high-altitude regions of Asia, Africa and South America. During the course of many expeditions, Tim has climbed new routes on a number of peaks including Gasherbrum IV and Everest.

Anthropologist **Seb Mankelow** has visited the Indian Himalaya on nine occasions since 1994, and has published papers on Ladakh's changing agricultural practices. Seb has also climbed and trekked in the Pamirs, Alaska, Yukon, East Africa and Nepal.

In the course of about 3000 mountain trips, **Reinhold Messner** has chalked up some one hundred first ascents and was the first person to climb all the world's 8000-metre peaks. The author of 40 books, he is currently a European parliamentarian.

A seasoned alpinist, **Dr John Mitchell** is a practising emergency physician in Cambridge and is also board certified in primary care. John has undergone training in tropical medicine and remote health care, and has practised medicine in several countries, including Nigeria and Indonesia.

An explorer and maker of adventure travel documentaries for BBC radio, **John Pilkington's** programmes include *The*

Uttermost Part of the Earth about Patagonia and *On the Trail of Butch and Sundance* based in Bolivia.

The author of *The Unwritten Places* as well as numerous guidebooks to France and Greece, **Tim Salmon** recently completed a solo walk along the Paris Meridian from Dunkirk to the Pyrenees.

In addition to trekking in Nepal, **Glenn Shaw** has made several attempts to cross Canada's Continental Divide using huskies. Glenn suffers from 'brittle bones' and has been confined to a wheelchair (or 'snowmobile', as Glenn calls his custom-built vehicle) all of his life.

Rebecca Stephens was the first British woman to climb Everest and also the seven continental summits. An author and television presenter, Rebecca regularly writes and lectures about her experiences.

If Mallory did not reach the summit then **Jon Tinker** was the first Englishman to climb Everest from the north. He has survived winter expeditions to Everest and K2, and currently organises programmes for an adventure travel company

Since joining expeditions to Annapurna and Everest in the 1980s, **Henry Todd** has become a familiar face on the 8000ers as the organiser of commercial climbing expeditions.

Fire officer **Darren Tulley** has joined expeditions to the Pamirs and the Andes, and climbed in the USA and Alps.

After five years in the French Alps, alpine climber **Mark Twight** returned to the Alaska Range in 2000, where with Scott Backes and Steve House he climbed the Czech Direct on Denali in 60 hours. He is the author of *Extreme Alpinism*.

The first Briton to climb Everest without bottled oxygen (and by a new route) **Stephen Venables** has climbed in the Himalaya, Karakoram, Africa and South America. The author of several books, Stephen has won the Boardman Tasker Award for mountain literature.

Steve Watkins is a freelance photographer and writer. The co-author of several guidebooks, Steve currently gets his kicks from adventure racing.

Since his first trek in Kashmir in 1970, **Garry Weare** has covered more than 20,000km of trails in the Indian Himalaya. He is the author of Lonely Planet's *Trekking In the Indian Himalaya*.

Photographic Index

Index

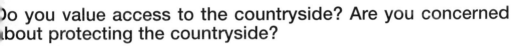

 act
access &
conservation
trust

Do you value access to the countryside? Are you concerned about protecting the countryside?

yes? then ACT is for you

Our ethos

Based in the UK, the ACCESS & CONSERVATION TRUST (ACT) is unique in focussing on the cliff and mountain environment and the needs of climbers, hillwalkers and mountaineers. Established as a charity its focus is to provide sustained and sustainable access to cliffs, mountains and open countryside. It aims to:

- **Support** rural access and conservation projects that protect access and promote sustainable use of these areas

- **Educate** and raise awareness and understanding of conservation and responsible conduct issues

- **Inform** people about rural access and conservation issues

- **Research** the benefits and impacts of mountain recreation and tourism

- **Train** and support access volunteers

How will ACT make a difference?

- ACT will support larger projects with greater financial contributions

- Projects will focus on the sustainable use and conservation of the outdoor environment

Whatever your reasons, access and conservation of cliffs, mountains and open countryside benefits you as an individual. For more details or to make a pledge today **T: (0161) 445 4747**

GROUP LEADER INSTRUCTION IN THE UPLANDS

IMPROVING PUBLIC TRANSPORT IN THE COUNTRYSIDE

CHOUGHS – AN IMPORTANT CLIFF-NESTING BIRD PROTECTED FROM DISTURBANCE DURING THE NESTING PERIOD

access & conservation today for
freedom tomorrow

Access & Conservation Trust

77–179 Burton Road Manchester M20 2BB. Tel: (0161) 445 4747 Fax: (0161) 445 4500
E: info@accesstrust.co.uk W: www.accesstrust.co.uk

BMC

Insurance you can TRUST

Good reasons to choose
BMC Insurance

- Simple and easy to purchase
- Immediate professional service
- Worldwide 24 hour helplines
- 10 point customer service charter
- 3-day to annual cover
- UK, Europe or Worldwide cover
- Cover available for many sports including hill walking, trekking, climbing, and skiing
- Medical, search and rescue, repatriation and baggage cover come as standard with no hidden extras
- Comprehensive and excellent value for money

Over 50,000

hill walkers, climbers and mountaineers put their trust in the **British Mountaineering Council** to provide expert advice, services and information on the outdoors.

BMC Insurance is designed by experts to give you reassurance and peace of mind wherever you travel. All our quality policies are designed to be free from unreasonable exclusions or restrictions.

What's more all surpluses from **BMC** services are invested in work that promotes your interests and protects your freedoms – *so the only one to profit is you.*

Get your free copy of the
**BMC Travel & Activity
Insurance Guide**

INSTANT COVER

0161 445 4747
www.thebmc.co.uk

fax: 0161 445 4500 email: insure@thebmc.co.uk

**British Mountaineering
Council
Member Services
FREEPOST MR9759
Manchester M20 7AD**

THE HELLY HANSEN
NATIONAL
MOUNTAINEERING
EXHIBITION

**A SPLENDID ADVENTURE
JUST OFF THE M6**

FEATURES:
**WORLD EXCLUSIVE
MALLORY COLLECTION**

The Helly Hansen
National Mountaineering Exhibition
Tel: 01768 868000 www.mountain-exhibition.co.uk

Rheged – the Village in the Hill, Near Penrith, Cumbria
(Signposted from Juction 40 M6)

BMC

The BMC Travel Club: Free Introductory Membership

A unique opportunity to benefit from a range of BMC services and products. The Travel Club is for trekkers and mountaineers about to head out on their mountain journey. The benefits are tailored with just that in mind.

Just fill in the form below, tear off the card and post it back to the BMC and you will become a member of the Travel Club for the next three months. At the end of this period you will get an opportunity to apply for full BMC membership.

For the mountain traveller the benefits of membership are:

• Access to the members-only BMC Travel Insurance Service: unbeatable cover, designed by experts.

• Access to the BMC Travel Information Service: free information sheets to anywhere in the world and big discounts off Info Service publications.

• Discounts on other travel products direct from the BMC and from quality retailers.

• Free copy of the BMC's Summit magazine, membership card and new members pack.

So that's it: A free membership and you can use it to save loads of money. Makes sense?

Name...

Address..

....

....

Email...

Date..

21

British Mountaineering Council

Travel Club

Freepost MR9759

Manchester

M20 7AD